Ebdon's Odyssey

JOHN EBDON

Ebdon's Odyssey

Illustrations by
Michael ffolkes

PETER DAVIES : LONDON

Peter Davies Limited
10 Upper Grosvenor Street, London W1X 9PA

LONDON   MELBOURNE   TORONTO
JOHANNESBURG   AUCKLAND

Copyright © 1979 by John Ebdon
First published in Great Britain 1979

432 04020 X

Printed and bound in Great Britain by
Morrison & Gibb Ltd, London and Edinburgh

TO
JOHN MAQUISOS,
MY FRIENDS IN THE ISLANDS
OF
ANDROS AND KOS
AND
'MARIA'

ΣΤΟΝ
ΓΙΑΝΝΗ ΜΑΡΚΟΥΪΖΟ
ΣΤΟΥΣ ΦΙΛΟΥΣ ΜΟΥ ΣΤΑ ΝΗΣΙΑ
ΑΝΔΡΟ ΚΑΙ ΚΩ
ΚΑΙ ΣΤΗΝ
'ΜΑΡΙΑ'

Contents

Illustrations

Acknowledgements

John Morgan Travel
Timsway Travel
Triton Holidays, Rhodos
Michael Wheen, Esqre.

Introduction

This book is about Greece. It is not a travel book. It is about people: those of my own country who crashed into my life during my journeys, but primarily about the men and women of two villages in the islands of Andros and Kos; people with unsophisticated tastes, living uncomplicated lives. It was amongst them and through them that I fell in love with Greece.

PART ONE

CHAPTER I

Myths and Matrons

IT WAS ELEVEN years ago that I first set foot on Greece. I
did so with two hundred preparatory school boys and an
equal number of geriatrics who formed the other half of what
was advertised as an Educational Cruise. I broke away from
them at Corinth, where we debussed in order to allow the
wise and intellectually orientated of both age groups to take in
food for thought and the less prudent and philistine of the
mature to drink ouzo in the midday sun.

I admit to masochistic tendencies. In 1975 I accepted a similar
offer to join another cruise ship. Once again Greece was
included in the itinerary. Mykonos, Delos and Crete were
visited with indecent but necessary haste; the historic sites of
the latter two were toured with hysterical speed, and sponges
were bought at the former.

It was a 'Discovery' cruise. For the uninitiated this is a type
of voyage to which personalities of varying degrees of notoriety
or expertise are invited to act as targets for the fare-paying
passengers. Lured by the prospect of free meals, cheap drinks
and brochure-blue skies and unmindful that they will be in
need of urgent psychiatric attention on their return, the unwary

or impecunious accept the invitation. Which is why I was aboard. I was there to be discovered. And I was.

Within an hour of embarking there was an imperious knock on my cabin door. Looking up from my suitcase I was confronted by a mountain of tartan. The Edinburgh Matron had entered my life. She was totally resistible. Large, Jenner-clad and sensibly shod, she belonged to that intimidating ilk who are born behatted and ordained to preside at bridge parties. 'I know what I like,' their faces say as they emerge from the womb, 'and it's not much.'

For a moment she eyed me in silence and thinly veiled hostility. Then, in the incisive accent of Princes Street, she said: 'Oo! Oo soo that's what you look laike! Dear me, what a pity. Aid arlways imegined you quaite def'rently but never maind it can't be helped; noo.'

'Yes,' she went on with the insensitivity of a steam roller, 'Ai got your cebin from the Pussers Bu-roh just now. Quaite frenkly Ai thart he was a wee bet impairtinent becos he said "Well," he said, "I doubt ef he's finished unpecking yet", but Ai said, never maind about that – after arl he's paid to be abard is he not? But anyway,' she continued with growing disapproval, 'Ai've often heard you on the wireless and wondered why you were. Yes, it's what Ai call a non-progrum. Yes. Not that Aim without humour of cos – in fect mai late harsbond, he's dead of cos, mai late harsbond used to say he found me quaite droll, in a whimsical way.'

Fifteen minutes later she departed leaving me marvelling at her husband's perception and filled with disquiet for the days ahead. Fortunately for me she found other fish to fry. Without exception all the deck officers aged prematurely during the next forty-eight hours.

It was not until we reached Mykonos some days later that I received her undivided attention again. There, as we waited with three hundred other passengers to be taken in small boats to the nearby island of Delos, an elderly Greek on the quayside plucked a tune for us from the strings of an equally old bouzoukoi. For a long moment she bore with him. Then, with the grouse feather in her hat rampant with chauvinism, she proclaimed: 'Pairsonally Ai prefar the paipes.'

She was a remarkable woman. For the first part of the forty-minute journey to the island she straddled the centre of the boat like an army of occupation. Stern faced and with arms akimbo she frowned into the distance beyond the prow, but when we were about halfway to Delos she suddenly turned downwind and declaimed to the Cyclades in general and me in the particular.

'The Aisles of Greece, the Aisles of Greece where barning Seppho larved and seng! Ah yes,' she bellowed reminiscently, 'mai late harsbond used to spik that beautifully, that and the waine dark sea bit – he was a vet you know.' And then before I could fathom the tenuous connection between Homer, Sappho and the veterinary service she said: 'Maithology! You'd be interested in that, of cos? Of cos. You've bin to Delos before of cos? Noo? Oo! Oo what a pity. Ai hev, three taimes since mai harsbond dade – garlstones you know.'

'Yes,' she continued, 'it's arfly worth whaile. The Lions, you know about the Lions of cos? The stoon Lions? They're arfly good; considering their age; so are the phalluses – some of the best Ai've seen in fect. *And* Ai've seen a great many. Which reminds me,' she said reflectively, and with the suspicion of wistfulness, 'Ai do hope we get the same guide as we had the last time – he was arfly good, arfly informative; particularly about Apollo; his mother-in-law lives in Stoke-on-Trent.'

She paused briefly to adjust her hat pin. Then in the manner of one delivering an ultimatum she said: 'Ai suppose you realize that Apollo was not breast-fed? Noo? Oo. Oo well it's not

5

surprising I suppose, but he was not. Noo! Never given suck in his laife – it was arl nectar and ambrosia from the spoon. I got that from the guide last time – he really was arfly good – arfly good.'

As I said, she was a remarkable woman for whom no tourist venue in Greece remained untrod; but the fates were kind to her that day – we did get her guide.

As we drifted the last few yards to our mooring place I saw a tall, slim, broadly smiling man with many teeth and a Pythagoran moustache, standing a little apart from the welcoming committee of Delos; and so did the Edinburgh Matron. A tremor of excitement disturbed her tweeds.

'Oo!' she said, clutching my arm with one hand and pointing a quivering finger with the other, 'that's him, that's the one! Oo how fartunate, how *arfly* fartunate! Ai just can't wait to plunder his brain again, I just cannot wait!'

Nor did she. First ashore and leaving a trail of wounded and bruised behind her, she bounded toward him like a hippo on heat panting with exertion and anticipation. 'Oo!' she roared as she advanced, 'Oo, *what* a surpraise, *what* a fartunate heppening! Oo the things Ai want to ask you! You remember me of cos from last time? Well of cos you do, what a stupid question – silly me!'

For a second the sparkle went out of his eyes and teeth simultaneously and a look of intense strain, if not of horror, replaced the smile. He swallowed hard.

'Ah yes,' he said hoarsely and with the air of a condemned man, as the awful truth dawned upon him, 'how are you do?' And, he added insincerely, 'Welcome back. But now I speak to all the peoples. Lady and gentlemens,' he said, raising his voice and taking the opportunity to draw away from her, 'please to follow me to the first ruin to hear my speech of information.'

'*The Aisles of Greece, the Aisles of Greece . . .*'

Hercules – improbably that was his name – was a complete professional; and he was 'arfly good'. In the discourse which was to follow, his enthusiasm for his country's mythology was undeniable but what filled me with joy was the freshness of his approach to the subject. Not for him the formalized style so beloved by many of our senior lecturers on classical history who, peering through their bifocals, first at their papers and then at their audiences, deliver their offerings in unenthusiastic tones as dry as moon dust.

'Well ladies and gentlemen,' they would have begun, removing and polishing their spectacles in a well tried gambit and repeating the gesture at intervals throughout the peroration, 'as you are aware, this island of Delos is one of the smaller ones in the Cyclades, or, if you so prefer, the *Kyk*lades – or even the Kykl*a*des and the one on which Apollo and Artemis reputedly – reputedly mark you, reputedly – were born of Zeus and Leto, whose history and genealogy is, as you well know, to be found in Hesiod's poem "The Theogony" written in about the eighth century BC – or so some would have it – and whose characteristic physiognomy, traditional attitudes and time-honoured legends appear together with those of the many other divinities of which the Greek pantheon was composed in the Iliad and Odyssey of Homer.' And so on. But not Hercules.

Standing tall upon a vantage point on the ruins of a temple and facing an audience of stone lions and the assembled multitude, he raised his arms for quiet. 'Shoosh,' said the Edinburgh Matron severely to those around her, 'shoosh! Shoosh-shoosh!' We shooshed.

In silence Hercules looked around him. The day was his. He took a deep breath. Then in a voice roughened with retsina and rakki he roared: 'Lady and Gentle –'. Unexpectedly his voice went up an octave and squeaked into obscurity. 'Oo dear,' said the Edinburgh Matron, 'Oo dear, dear, dear! Oo dear, dear, dear, dear, dear – hev a sweetie!'

Hercules shook his head and with intense concentration coaxed an enormity from the back of his throat and spat toward a stone lion. 'Better,' he said and, lowering his voice to a bellow, began again. 'Lady and gentlemens, this here is the birthing place of Apollon – Apollo to you. Apollo who was borned from the sperma of Zeus.'

Near by a lady from Sutton Coldfield shifted uneasily on her stone seat.

'Zeus!' continued our mentor, 'Zeus! Aha! I tell you something about him, not half I do not: he was very good with the girls! And not only goddess girls but human girls as well. He liked all girls and,' he added, giving full value to each word, 'he . . . was . . . very . . . strong.' At this juncture he leered happily, bent dramatically at the knees and placing his left arm on his right arm jerked the limb slowly upward. 'You know what I mean' he said.

A worldly middle-aged quorum assured him that they understood him perfectly. So too, in the unstable tones of puberty, did a thirteen-year-old boy. His parents looked at him with some concern; and then, with deeper anxiety, at each other. The lady from Sutton Coldfield inhaled sharply and began a meticulous examination of her finger nails.

Warmed and encouraged by the majority decision, Hercules plunged deeper into the pool of rhetoric and endorsed his previous statement.

'Zeus,' he said, 'was – fantastic! Do you know, lady and gentlemens, about the Tit-ans? What? All right – *Titons.* Thank you, thank you very much. *Titons.* Well one Tit-ones. stayed with him nine nights and then birth-ed nine daughters Nine daughter, lady and gentlemens – she had hell of a time. And,' he added pontifically, 'serve her right.'

'Yeah,' said an American voice, 'some broad.'

'These nine daughter,' continued Hercules, now sure of his audience, 'were the Muses. The Muses. But now, lady and gentlemens, I make a joke – she was not, a-mused! Ha! Ha!' He clapped his hands in encouragement. 'Yes! Thank you, thank you very much! Like your Queen Victoria I think! Yes! My wife tell me that; she comes from – Stokontrent. And,' he added, 'she is pregnant!' The applause was deafening. 'Atta boy,' said the man from Detroit. 'So,' Hercules summarized, 'Zeus was very good in the beds. And now we talk about Apollo.'

Back in England several graves at Balliol opened in anticipation.

'Apollo,' said Hercules, 'all right, lady and gentlemens he was very beautiful and handsomes man and good with his bow and arrows and make lovely music, but' – and here he paused – 'no-good-with-the-girls!'

The lady from Sutton Coldfield began a detailed exploration of her hand bag.

Hercules looked at her. 'Please do not misunderstand me,' he said, and extended his arms in appeal. 'He wanted – but they wouldn't! For hexample he liked very much the water nymphs. Some live in salt water, some live in fresh water and some live in stagnant water. Well, Apollo he didn't much like the salt nymphs or stagnant nymphs but he like very much one called Daphne. You heard of her?' he inquired.

The pubic one nodded enthusiastically.

'Good,' said Hercules. 'Well she live in the river and he chase her like mad but just as he was about to ravage her the earth split open, she fell through and Apollo was furious because where she wasn't there was a laurel tree and you can imagine what was his feeling; and that was the sort of luck he had and often it is like that I think with handsome men.'

'Yeah,' said the man from Detroit, inaccurately assessing the situation, 'Poofs.'

'And now, lady and gentlemens,' said Hercules, 'before we go hon are there any questions about Apollo?'

There was a pregnant silence. And then just as I was wondering if Apollo's little sadnesses were the result of his not being breast-fed, the day was made for me. The voice of Sutton Coldfield broke the stillness with three words: 'Disgusting,' it said, 'quite disgusting.'

If Hercules heard the outburst he treated it with Stoic indifference; but not so the Edinburgh Matron.

"To the pure,' she said loudly, 'arl is pure.'

She turned to me with a look of triumph. 'Did Ai not say he was good? Is he not a maine of information?' I nodded. 'And,' she bellowed, regardless that Hercules was but three yards from us, 'have you noticed his teeth? And the way he moves from the heps?'

I shook my head. 'Oo he does,' she said, 'he does, he does! But then they arl do, you know – until they go to fet that is. Have you noticed thet – how the Greeks go to fet? Not surpraising of cos when you think of their cooking. Have you hed Greek fud? Swim-ming in oil it is, swim-ming in it.' She breaststroked her way through the phrase and continued.

'Ai remember once going into a rest'rant in Ethens with mai harsbond – it was some years bek now, before he was claimed – and ordering a dish of something or other – Ai can not remember what it was but it was Greek, and it was just swim-ming in oil. And Ai said, "Noo," Ai said. "Take thet away," Ai said, "and bring me something plain." And the garlic. Oo dear, oo dear, oo dear! Tch, tch, tch, tch, tch!' Her dentures chattered with indignation. 'Of cos thet's why they smell! Have you nooticed thet, the way they smell? At least they do to me. Of cos mai harsbond used to say it's an aphrodisiac –

not that he ever had any of cos – I wouldn't have had him in
the house if he had; but they're nice people when you get to
know them.' For a moment I had a fear that she would turn
directly to Hercules and say, 'Aren't you?' And give him a pat.
Mercifully she did not.

Grasping him energetically by the lapels and with her eyes
glistening she shouted: 'And now we goo to the Phallus do
we not?' He nodded.

'Follow me,' he rasped, and shepherding the rest of the flock,
including the lady from Sutton Coldfield who, although still
in a state of shock, had obviously come to the conclusion that
she might as well be hung for a sheep as a lamb, set off with her
hard on his heels.

As I dropped behind, on the pretext of lighting my pipe, I
reflected how unfortunate it is that so many tourists abroad
presume that all the indigenous population with whom they
have contact are either hard of hearing and must be bellowed
at, or stone deaf and therefore insensible of anything said in
front of them.

The other thought to occupy me as I wandered in the
tourist wake, still mindful of the Matron's exposé on Greek
dietetics, was the distrust and fear which so many British have
of foreign food. This thought remained with me for the rest of
our short stay on Delos and indeed was fed during the return
journey to Mykonos by the discovery of a small publication
in the ferry entitled 'Greek and How to Speak it'. I have no
idea to whom of my companions it belonged for no one claimed
it, but clearly it was the property of an apprehensive dyspeptic.
On a much-thumbed page in the otherwise unmarked book
were the phrases: 'I am on a diet'; 'I do not want anything
with garlic, meat, fish in it'; 'This does not smell very nice';
'This has too much fat' and 'Without oil, salt, sugar, gravy,
please'.

To be fair, it was a very good little book. Having offered those invaluable sentences as an aid to preserving the status quo of one's stomach it did not assume that success would come automatically. Immediately following the list, which was headed 'General Difficulties', were the telling phrases – 'I have left my glasses, my watch and my ring in the toilet' and, most ominous of all, 'I have been here for some time' . . . patently the publication was compiled by an experienced realist.

Nevertheless it depressed me. What, I asked myself, had happened to the spirit of adventure for which our nation was once renowned? But I need not have worried. Within an hour of our return to Mykonos I saw one of Britain's stalwarts in action. He was an elderly Englishman and he was having the best of three falls with a piece of genuine Turkish Delight. It was a macabre spectacle.

It is not generally realized but the indigenous variety of Turkish Delight bears no resemblance to that proffered in English restaurants with the coffee – that one may eat without having to disappear under the table to do running repairs. The real article however not only has an adhesive property that beggars all description, but a will of its own, and when genuine Turkish Delight encounters genuine National Health dentures the result has to be seen to be believed.

As far as I can recollect the gentleman in question ended up with his back braced against the wall going puce in the face and saying '*Nnnnnnng*'; or words to that effect. Eventually, and after what to him must have seemed several centuries, there was a sound which I associated with the hurried exit of the very last of the bath water. '*Schluck*', he said, and again, '*Schluck*'. Then, as I watched, a parabola of white, pink-coated with Delight, arched its way high into the air, gleaming and glistening in the Mykonos sun and finally clattered to the ground in front of him. In a fixed and silent grin, his teeth rested, mocking him. On reflection I can quite understand why page 130 in the phrasebook ended with the entry: 'I have broken my plate, can you repair it?'

Shortly after that incident we sailed for Crete. I for one was not sorry to leave Mykonos – it is a spoilt island; and nor was the Edinburgh Matron. She appeared at the quayside clasping a monstrous and obscene sponge. 'Hev you eaten?' she asked, 'Ai hev *and* Ai paid through the noose! Forty drekmy for some cheese with a wee bit of origanum on it *and* Ai could not get tea either. But still,' she added, pointing to her sponge, 'Ai did get this arfly cheap, arfly competitive it was. Ai shall enjoy it in mai bath – once the smell's gone, thet is, but what to do with it the meanwhile Ai just don't knoo.'

At her elbow the short gentleman from Detroit who shared a table with her aboard offered her some terse and totally impractical advice from the corner of his mouth.

She looked down at him coldly over the sponge. 'Thet,' she said, 'was arfly coarse.'

Providentially I saw nothing of her during the hours we were at sea. She did not appear at dinner and rumour had it that she had either succumbed to cheese poisoning or had been attacked by her sponge, but whatever the reason for her absence, massed prayers of thanks were offered by her table companions for their unexpected deliverance. However she was in evidence again by the time we reached Crete the following morning and set off in Coach Number 33. It was upon that island that the performance of Hercules on Delos was totally eclipsed by one given in the ruins of Knossos by a stumpy lady with smoked glasses and a larynx to match.

In an accent suggesting that her pronunciation of English was the result of alternating sojourns in Belgravia and Shepherds Bush she opened her account of Minoan civilization thus: 'Now! Number Tarty Tree! Ceuch Tarty Tree? Yeu are

all 'ere? Bekorse Ai deun't tark until yeu are hall 'ere. Gude!
'Now probablee yeu are warndering whai this charmbah is
sew lew deaun. Well Ai terl yeu. It is bekorse 'ere we are
souffering mooch from the wind. And even all theuse yars ageu
they souffered from the wind. Even the King. And this is his
charmbah in which he spend much taime. Yaas!... and now
we geu to the queen's behind ... seu follow please ...'
    We followed: 'Seu! Number Tarty Tree – yeu are all 'ere
agene? Gude! Seu now we are in the Queen's charmbah. This
was her barth-rume, her, Dooble-yu-see as you maight say;
whar she is habluting. You understand? Gude.
    'Now please to neutice the barths, the shape of the barths
bekorse not eunly are they being used for barths but also for
sar-koo-fou-garses – coffins. You understand? Gude. First
they are habluting in them and then finally they was adjusted
in the fatal position. You understand? Now ...'
    I do not know what the Edinburgh Matron thought of that
guide, but her teeth were not of the first order and she did not
move from the hips. Nor did I find out. Shortly before the end
of the cruise we broke off diplomatic relations. At Dubrovnik.
But I can remember my paramount thought. The next time
I visit the Aegean, I pondered, by all the gods on Olympus I
shall do so independently.
    My thoughts were not conditioned by nationalism. I have
nothing against Caledonians, whatever their sex or size. Nor
do I dispute the value of cruises of the kind I have described.
Without doubt they fulfil a need for many; but not for me. In
my experience not only does the cruise and the organized tour
attract large ladies who have lost their husbands through
natural causes, carelessness or design, and other tiresome
itinerants, but retinues of sales folk to boot. I do not begrudge
them their pickings but I like neither them nor the haunts
where they hunt: one cannot see the real face of Greece

through a plethora of plastic worry beads and Delphic shirts hot from the looms of Lancashire.

However, I returned to England grateful for my experience. Not only had the voyage afforded me the opportunity of observing my fellows at play and established beyond doubt what I knew already, namely that we are a funny crowd – especially aboard and abroad – but it had strengthened my resolve to see non-tourist Greece as soon as possible. My appetite was whetted and I dreamed of simple pensions in little towns and villages on unfashionable islands. And dreams they remained until I met a man who helped to turn them to reality.

His name was John Philippedes and I met him at a party in Drayton Gardens, London S.W.1. He spoke a peculiar brand of English but came, he said, from the island of Andros in the Cyclades. We took to each other immediately and the sharing of a common Christian name helped the relationship. I told him of my wishes and my dislikes. 'Ah yes,' he said, 'I ham understanding of your unloves – I have had the rips off in this country.'

His description of Andros enthralled me. It was, I gathered, three hours' sail from the mainland, and Hora the capital, the town where he lived, was almost unknown to the tourist. 'For my opinion,' he said, 'you must go there, Yanni. For my opinion,' he repeated, 'it is, how to say – right up your passage.'

It was a good party. In the small hours of the following morning we exchanged addresses, swore eternal friendship and went our unsteady ways into the pink and grey of a London dawn. We were next to meet two months later under a darkening sky, in Andros.

CHAPTER II

Plumbing and Philippedes

'AIRPORTS,' WROTE A romantic and, I suspect, slightly deranged travel journalist, 'are full of magic.' She was, of course, entitled to her opinion; one writes what one feels. Personally I have always found that departure lounges in general and that of Gatwick in particular are innocent of that quality. At any time. And when one is confined within them for four and a half hours after one's scheduled take-off the sense of enchantment is even more elusive.

It was in such an unhappy situation that I found myself at the beginning of an autumn journey to Andros; I was less than euphoric when eventually we did become airborne and I watched dawn breaking over Crawley instead of the Aegean. Nor did my feeling of bonhomie increase when the young woman sitting next to me in the aircraft poured her scalding coffee between my thighs.

'Oh goodness,' she said, as I hit top C and my knuckles turned white, 'Oh gosh, I *am* sorry, I am honestly, hon*est*ly I am, I am *really*.' She was a well brought up girl and I did not doubt her sincerity.

As I made my way toward the rear of the plane as if holding

an imaginary cello between my legs, my progress was watched with prurient curiosity by a keen-eyed and disgusting small boy. When I was within four rows of him he turned to his mother, giggled, and whispered something. Startled, she lowered her copy of the *Nursing Mirror* and looked up. 'No,' she said, 'of course he hasn't.' But her voice lacked conviction.

It was an unpleasant journey. Everything that could go wrong did so and continued so to do from Athens onward. There, I was to have been met by a close friend: needless to say I was not. There are limits for even close friends. Instead I found a cryptic note which read: 'Sorry old boy – gone bed (you know what Vanda's like) take taxi bs stn – 15 mins 30 drachs – ask Rafina Love M.'

Forty-five minutes and one hundred drachmae later I reached the bus station for Rafina; and it was there that I was taught two salutary lessons. I learned that while the Greeks are a very kind, warm and hospitable people they are also just the tiniest bit unreliable. Secondly, I came to know that they are great exponents of the Biblical maxim 'the last shall be first'. Especially at bus queues. It took me some time to realize this last important fact of Grecian life, but I am proud to say that after I had watched the first bus pull away and recovered from a variety of superficial wounds I did deadheat for second place in the next vehicle, having at one time been fourteenth in the field. Unfortunately my victory, like that enjoyed by the late King Pyrrhus, proved costly.

Shortly after I had started to lay about me with my suitcase and claimed three maimed and one winded, I was approached by a charming young man who said to me in a mixture of mime and Greek:

'Excuse me, you cannot take that case inside with you – I will put it on top of the bus.' With the wisdom of hindsight a more accurate translation would have been: 'I will put it on top of the bus – if I remember.' I make mention of this because after I had embussed and we were some two hundred yards from the bus station, a stout West African gentleman who had been observing the receding landscape keenly through the rear window was suddenly galvanized into anguished action.

'Stop-de-coach!' he said hoarsely and emotionally. 'Stop-de-coach! Stop-de-coach-immediately-I-say! My bloody-damn-baggage is not with me!' It was a very moving scene and not unlike Medea's farewell to her children.

Despite the language barrier, miraculously the message reached the driver. The bus screeched to a halt in a cloud of burning rubber from what laughingly were known as its tyres, the West African one catapulted from the rear door and legged it for all he was worth in the direction of de-bloody-damn-baggage, and those occupants of the coach who had not been crippled by its sudden stop gave him a rousing cheer. And then off we went again.

For a matter of seconds I watched his retreating figure until he vanished round a bend in the road, musing on his misfortune and then – and with a horrible clarity and a speed matching that of St Paul's conversion on the road to Damascus, the realization came to me that if the Third World's baggage was adrift mine could be also. So the pantomime was re-enacted and once again Greek voices met in a mixed chorus of pain, blasphemy, jeers and cheers as I, too, made a premature exit. Thirty minutes later, weary and footsore, I reached the bus station in time to see my case being hoisted to the top of another vehicle; its destination lay in the opposite direction to mine. But I did get to Andros that day – by the last ferry, and it says much for Anglo-Greek relations that my friend Philippedes was still waiting for me at the port of Gavrion five hours after my anticipated arrival on the island.

'Yanni!' he said, throwing his arms wide in a superb gesture of extravagant welcome and drawing me within them, 'Yanni! Yasas Yasas, so long, so long – let me have the splendid look at you!' He held me at arms' length; and paused. 'My God! Yanni,' he said, 'for my opinion you look disastrous – not, for my opinion, very tasteful . . .'

There is nothing quite so comforting as being in the hands of friends when one is feeling hot and flyblown and it was with joy that I sank into the back seat of Philippedes's car; and stuck to it. Philippedes beamed at me from the front. 'Ah Yanni,' he said, 'now we begin our short journey, yes? Yes, I think so.' He pressed the starter and the car leapt forward into the back of another as cars will when they are left in gear. 'Yes,' said Philippedes quite unperturbed and backing into the front of the one parked to his rear. 'Yes, short but very beautiful – so much sea to view, so much hills to see, so much – how to say, exquarsite glories to notice and even now in the twoolight you will see them – yes, yes, I will remark upon them as I drove.'

He did so unceasingly for the first four miles. Nothing escaped his attention except the road and other traffic. Pointing from left to right and sometimes in both directions simultaneously and only occasionally showing annoyance over the intrusion of the steering wheel, he kept up a non-stop commentary as we steered an erratic course toward the east coast of the island and to the village of Niborio where I was to stay. I had reasoned that we should reach it before dark, but that was before my discovery that Philippedes's driving was as unusual as his English; now I began to have doubts about whether we should arrive at all.

My thoughts must have been communicated to Philippedes. 'Yanni,' he said, suddenly taking both hands from the wheel and raising them in apology, 'I talk too much and you are tired, but soon you will be in the bed – now I keep the quiet for you until we arrive.' We drove on in silence and for the first time in hours I started to relax. I began to think longingly of the pension which awaited me at journey's end.

Arrangements for this accommodation had been made by a mutual friend of Philippedes and myself who had written: 'I warmly recommend Arianna Grammatikakis's villa. It's up a small hill overlooking the bay and although I haven't been there for ages it will offer you the following advantages: a very friendly and sympathetic landlady, an open fire for the autumn evenings, unlimited hot water and a splendid sunken Roman-type bath for sporting in.' And then he had added a postscript which read: 'As I remember the bedrooms are a little on the small side.'

One thing about my friend, and it is politic that he should remain nameless, he does have an extraordinarily retentive memory. Agreed, as I was to discover, his recollection of the Roman bath was perhaps a little clouded unless he had some incredibly small Romans in mind, because even Romulus and Remus in their early infancy would have found it difficult to disport themselves in it. With or without the soap. Personally I would have described it as a sheep dip. For stunted Merinos. But, to be charitable, even Homer may nod.

He was, however, correct in his assessment of the bedrooms. They were a little on the small side. Or to put it another way: until I stayed in Grammatikakis's establishment I had never slept in a room with a wall to wall mattress. Come to that I had never before slept upon a bed from which I could close the door of the room without having to leave it in order to do so. It afforded me a remarkable experience and one which gave me a better understanding of why battery hens look so down in the beak at times.

My friend's reference to unlimited hot running water was also uncannily accurate. At least on the whole it was. If I want to cavil I would query his use of the words 'hot' and 'unlimited', but it certainly ran; and I am sure that had he known he would have added 'but seldom through the taps'. Through the ceiling and down the walls, yes – nobody could wish for greater efficiency – it was an unqualified success; but then I learned of the force of Greek water power from the moment I stepped from the car at the foot of the earth road leading up the hill to the Grammatikakis's villa. There, even in the twilight, I could see that I had been unwise not to pack my wellingtons. There was a gloss to that one-in-four gradient which filled me with disquiet. Moreover there was a sound for which I did not much care. And a smell.

Philippedes switched off the engine and joined me. 'So, Yanni!' he said, putting his arm around my shoulders, 'so, we are here, yes?'

'Yes,' I said, attempting to keep the surprise from my voice, 'Yes, we are.'

'And so now,' he continued, 'now really you begin your lovely holi-holiday.' He paused, his nostrils twitching in the fading light. 'Yanni,' he said, 'do you know something? In my nose there is a strange essence.' He sniffed the air inquiringly from left to right like a disbelieving bloodhound. Then as his other senses sharpened in the gathering night: 'Yanni,' he said, in a voice low with apprehension, 'Yanni, tell me please, tell me – can you hear booblings?'

'Booblings?' I asked.

'Yes,' he said, 'booblings, booblings. In my ear I hear booblings, very strange booblings, almost as if it was coming from the gro-ground.' He made a quick intake of breath. 'My God, Yanni,' he said, 'I tell you something; for my opinion Mrs Grammatikakis is having the troubles with her water! And this, Yanni, is a problem for, in my opinion, it will give her a headache!'

'Ah, poor girl,' I said, 'she gets headaches does she?'

'Yes,' said Philippedes, 'yes, yes, always the headaches, but now let us start ascending and I will tell you something about her for, in my opinion, she is a very strange woman, as you might say. Yes. She once endangered her stomach with a sandbag and – are your feet wet, Yanni? Yes, so are mine, and ever since then – so are my socks – ever since then she gets the headache when problems happen and then she, and then she – Yanni!' His voice took on a fresh urgency. 'Mind where you tread! Mind where . . . tch! tch! tch! Never mind, never mind, it will wash off later . . . so many dogs here . . . and then Yanni she goes to the bed or to Athens to see her head doctor. Yes, seekeeartrist, seekeeartrist, yes, yes, that is the word, yes! . . .' And so on.

I believe it was the poet Rupert Brooke, of blessed memory, inert church clocks and honey, who wrote:

> 'One may not doubt that, somehow, good
> shall come of water and of mud;
> And, sure the reverent eye must see
> A purpose in liquidity.'

He also eulogized, I remember, about river smells.

The top, when we reached it, short of breath and temper, was in total darkness; and silent.

'H'm,' said Philippedes, 'this is for my opinion, strange. But wait.' He walked over to the building silhouetted against the skyline and peered through a window. 'Most strange,' he reaffirmed, flattening his nose against the pane, 'there is only the darkness inside.' And rapped on the glass.

It was the signal for which the morgue had been waiting.

From somewhere in the house there was a suppressed scream. A main light was switched on, two dogs went berserk, and into a large stone-flagged and french-windowed room tripped a figure dressed remarkably like Isadora Duncan. She flitted at great speed all round the room, switching on lights: like the fairy queen scene in a pantomime, everything lit up as she touched it. She should, I thought, as I gazed in wonder, be holding a wand or be accompanied by tinkling bells. Then, as suddenly as it had begun, the whirlwind tour finished.

In a flow of chiffon Mrs Grammatikakis, for it was none other, danced to the french windows, flung them wide and laughed hysterically into the night. 'Kalispera!' she shrieked, 'Kalispera! Peraste! Peraste!'

So we did – we went in. Philippedes exchanged perfunctory pleasantries with her and then introduced me. She turned her head toward me and blinked rapidly for some seconds.

'Ha-ha-ha!' she said; and twitched. Then, turning back to Philippedes she spoke to him quickly and intensely.

Damp, smelly and untasteful, and with the dogs looking at me with undisguised loathing, I waited for a translation of the diatribe which was taking place. Somehow I could sense that both Euripedes and Sophocles would have been gratified with the shaping of events.

Eventually Mrs Grammatikakis came to the end of her recital.

Philippedes said: 'Herumph! Yanni! As was my opinion, Mrs Grammatikakis has been to bed with her head and to-morrow she will go to Athens, very early in the morning, to visit her doctor so you will not see her. No. Also she does not wish you to be lonely so she is leaving her dogs with you and, for my opinion, already they like you very much. Yes. They will be your friends, your good friends, yes, yes, good do-aach!'

He sucked the back of his hand with enthusiasm. 'Also,' he continued, applying his handkerchief as a tourniquet, 'she wishes me to inform you that the hydro engineer will be here very early in the morning to fix her flow of water. Also, now, before she goes to the bed she wishes to demonstrate to you how to light the fire because she is sympathetic to you and does not wish you to be chilled in the night. It is very simple really – very, very simple, but she will show you now.' He paused and dramatically indicated that the moment of truth had arrived.

Mrs Grammatikakis giggled nervously, jetéed to the far side of the room, returned in a similar display of balletics with a can smelling strongly of petrol, removed the cap with a gesture worthy of Giselle, and waited expectantly for Philippedes to continue. He did so.

'As you can see,' he said, like a ringmaster presenting his pièce de résistance, 'the fireplace is full of logs, small, small logs, and that is some sort of benzine she is pouring on them . . . pouring on them and – arketá, Arianna, arketá, enough I think, yes. And now,' he concluded, 'we wait for ignition.'

Once more Mrs Grammatikakis went into her ballet routine.

I remember clearly the scrape of the match against the sand-papered box and seeing her toss it toward the fireplace, but after the initial explosion my memories are distinctly hazy. As I recollect, Mrs Grammatikakis took off in a shower of small, small logs and the dogs fled in the general direction of the mainland; but I did not see their mistress again that night. Nor did I see her in the morning. What I did see when I opened my eyes was a hairy arm reaching around my door and groping for a small green button set in the wall. Then, as I watched, hypnotized, the arm's owner sidled into view. He was small, tanned, and wore a gangrened beret.

'Ah!' he said, exhaling a cloud of day-old garlic. 'Aahh! Kalimera!' And then with ominous deliberation: 'I try to make water, on you.' And with that promise he pressed the button and went out of my life.

After a restless night in a waterless pension and having shared the same roof as two neurotic dogs with a predilection for human flesh, and a similarly deranged landlady, I was not at my best. As one in a coma I retained the sitting position into which I had been startled and tried to convince myself that the apparition was merely part of a nightmare and not tangible, unwanted flesh and blood; but I was not successful. Unfortunately one cannot ignore the lingering reality of garlic. And with this sad fact unpleasantly established, I crawled to the end of my bed, negotiated the two foot gap which separated it from the half open door and entered the adjoining box to my right. Optimistically but fraudulently it was called the bathroom. I was much in need of one of its services, meagre though they were. Even as a child I was unable to accept the more dramatic incidents in life with equanimity and manhood has made no difference to me in that respect. Also I wanted to think things out and I know of few places more conducive to constructive thought than bathrooms.

It was a strange cubicle. To my right was the sunken bath about which my anonymous friend had eulogized, and to which I referred earlier. Innocent of any trace of recent water it contained a quantity of used matches, three large spiders and a morose and very dry frog squatting by the plug hole; it eyed me lugubriously in sympathetic silence.

In front of me was a hand basin with a sepia crack running in an east-westerly direction across its bottom. Emblazoned under the overflow was the legend 'RELIANT', below which piece of braggadocio, albeit in smaller lettering, was the chauvinistic but rash addendum – 'Made in England'.

However, it was the walls which fascinated me. They were festooned with pipes. Unlike those in England which lie hidden in plastered modesty, these stood proudly against the whitewashed walls forming patterns on which even Dali would have found it difficult to improve – octopuses in conjugal embraces, mural Medusas, all were represented in one of the most

and a very dry frog

remarkable exhibitions of modern art I have ever seen on any wall, anywhere. But I was quite unprepared for what happened next.

One by one, the pipes burst into life. They began to mutter, one to the other. Conversations were struck up, punctured by flatulence. And then as the muttering grew to a rumbling so they became possessed, throbbing and pulsating in a riot of ecstasy as water surged through their leaden veins. Without warning the tap in the basin opposite to me blew off, and as the spiders dived for cover and the frog croaked a supplication to the ceiling, a jet of water like that from a sounding whale rose under me, forcing me to abandon the seat.

I know my breaking point. Within minutes of that incident I adjusted my dress in the accepted sense but without waiting to dry out, and aqua-planed from that sodden hell, past Grammatikakis's snarling guardians, and down the hill to safety. Half an hour later I squelched into Philippedes's office in the town.

John Philippedes, as I have indicated, is a very kind man with a working knowledge of the English language but an imperfect understanding of its syntax. He is also a very good man; but even his mother would own that he is not a good-looking man. In truth, when I was searching for the means to describe his features I came to a halt, for John Philippedes has no features. His face bears a striking resemblance to a rubber pantomime mask hung upon a wall after many hours of service. It droops. In short, it is a sagging face propped up by equine teeth with which nature richly has endowed him; but, to reiterate, he is a good and kind man and that morning he excelled in his generosity.

'Ah, Yanni!' he said when he had recognized the dishevelled heap before him, 'Kalimera! Kalimera! Kathiste! Kathiste! Yes, sit down, sit – no! No not there, please, because that is a good chair and – er I see the waters have come back to you. But no matter – soon you and your pants will change.

'Now, Yanni, tell me,' he continued, his composure recovered, 'tell me – did you sleep well last night?'

'Well,' I said, 'actually I didn't sleep at all.'

'No,' he said, looking more than ever like a fallen candidate at Becher's Brook, 'nor did I. Perhaps a quick wink and no more, because, Yanni, after I leave you at Grammatikakis's I was very mindful of your situation. In fact, Yanni, I am turning my wife over between winks and saying to her that for my opinion you are most disagreeable. And so, Yanni,' he went on, 'we are deciding that it would be more agreeable if you stay with us now tonight and tomorrow night. Then, because friends of my son will be filling this house to explosion, tomorrow's morrow, or even perhaps yesterday you stay as our guest in my cottage in Apikia village; then we find you a tasteful lodging in Niborio. And that will be good, yes?'

I nodded gratefully, uncaring of my inability to absorb his chronology. 'Good,' said Philippedes, 'splendid. You know Apikia, Yanni? Ah ha!' He lit a cigarette, exhaled, leaned back in his chair and clasped his hands behind his head.

'Apikia, Yanni,' he enlarged, 'is very beautiful. Very, very beautiful. That is where they are putting their water in bottles for refreshing livers as you might say.' He paused to let the information sink in. 'And there, Yanni, it is very peaceful. No dogs to bite you, no waters to flood on you when you wake up, just nothing but, how to say,' and here he searched for a phrase and regrettably found it, 'birds wind in the trees and song. Now can you imagine that, Yanni?'

I could. Only too clearly. Indeed my imagination ran riot at the thought of hearing what surely must be the most unusual dawn chorus in Europe. Furthermore, I could not help wondering perhaps whether the liver-refreshing water of

Apikia were not contributory to the birds' early morning
eccentricities; but I hope that such thoughts remained hidden.

Philippedes rose and stubbed out his half-smoked cigarette.
'And now,' he said, 'we go upstairs to the flat to meet Metaxia.
Then, when you have embraced, you plunge. Yes?'

'Yes,' I said obediently, 'I plunge.'

'And then, after your immersion, I think you sleep. Yes?'

'Yes,' I said with soggy gratitude, 'yes, I think I do.'

I did. Moreover not only did I plunge and sleep, but after
eating I plunged and slept again.

CHAPTER III

Prescotts in Paradise

SLEEP, TIME AND total immersion are wonderful healers. Early next morning I stood on the balcony of my room and looked down over the raked roofs of Hora, across the blue waters of the bay with its straggling village of Niborio and to the high green-wooded hills in the north-west. There, as Philippedes had pointed out to me the previous day, was Apikia; and it was to Apikia I resolved to walk that morning. It should, so Philippedes had promised me, take under an hour to reach the village proper and slightly less to a downhill track which led to his cottage on the outskirts. He had pencilled a rough guide for me, and armed with it I set off on the first of what was to be many excursions in that direction.

It is said that the first experience of anything is always poignant, the one to be most remembered, and certainly I recall that initial journey best of all.

As I left Niborio, with my back to the sea, I climbed steadily, following the road which ran like a tortured snake all the way to the village. At each turn the wind, never absent from the island, gusted stronger as I left the lee of a rockfaced corner and rounded the spur to face the short unprotected stretch ahead. To my left, boulder-strewn hillsides the colour of a flon's skin were prickly with gorse. On my right the road was lianked by a low, grey, stone wall below which the ground fell sharply away to a valley floor to rise again into more fertile hills; and beyond, smokeblue in the heat haze of a growing day, lay the mountains of Andros.

It was magnificent scenery, and as I climbed higher so the panorama became increasingly beautiful. Turning, I looked back at Niborio. The white dog's leg of the mole in the harbour seemed like a broken matchstick on the turquoise sea and the fishing boats in the little anchorage had become toys; yet the thin voices of their crews still reached me, carried up on the clear clean air. But one of the strongest memories I retain is that of the nestlings of villages which came into view as I halted and looked across the valley to the olive-treed slopes opposite.

Hamlets, that is all they were. Clusters of white and terracotta houses, each settlement graced with a tiny blue-domed church. Above them, single houses in irregular isolation peeped through the dark green ranks of cypress trees which marked the boundaries, and spotted the landscape with icing sugar pinks and whites. I remember thinking how the whole scene reminded me curiously of an Advent Calendar. Each day, I mused, I would open the door of a different house, and on Christmas Day, the church door. It was a childish conceit, I suppose, but it pleased me, and I stayed a long while in that one spot not only looking but seeing: William Davies's injunction to stand and stare was very strong and I did not reach Apikia that day. Instead I discovered the inestimable joy of being Time's master and not its slave. No longer was I harnessed to the hands of the clock, and I laughed aloud in exhilaration at my liberation. No rats race around the islands of Greece, and perhaps that is why the faces of the islanders are free from strain.

Eventually I came out of my reverie and went on my way, still climbing. A mile later, and still short of the village but able to pick out the track to Philippedes's cottage, I left the road and lunched. Apples and fetta cheese make good companions, especially when they are washed down with retsina kept cool in a Thermos flask. Nearby, hobbled goats grazed on the gorse. Occasionally they stopped in their feeding to look at me and make rude noises. For a while I tried to match the arrogance of their stares but it was an unequal contest: it was their territory and they knew it. Supremely content, I made a pillow of my haversack and stretched out on my back. Overhead the scavengers of Greece wheeled in blue-black spirals, watching and waiting for whatever the ground would offer. Around me the crickets sang; and insidiously the retsina went about its work . . .

Two hours later I awoke, my face burning from the unaccustomed sun. From the direction of Apikia came the faint sound of taped bouzoukoi music growing louder as the grocer's van from which it came drew nearer. I stood up and waved and it stopped in a cloud of dust and protesting brakes. A smiling face looked out from the driver's window.

'Herete!'

'Herete!'

'Anglos?'

'Ne, ime Anglos.'

'Ela! Come!'

A minute later we were corkscrewing our way down to Niborio and Hora.

'My God,' said Philippedes when he saw me, 'my God! Yanni, for my opinion, you are on heat . . .'

There were four of us at table that night. The lingua franca was English and it was used to relate all my misfortunes to Philippedes's son Spiros who was freshly arrived from Athens as the spearhead of the morrow's invasion by his friends from the mainland. Like his father he was an Anglophile, and as with his father his English was – interesting. Almost as interesting as my Greek.

Together we endeavoured to improve our respective knowledge of each other's language. Among other additions to my vocabulary they offered me various Greek toasts, 'Yasas! Kali orekse! Isighia!' and so on. In return I taught them 'Cheers! Chin chin! Here's to you! and Bottoms up!' Spiros was particularly enamoured of 'Bottoms up'; I could see that it captured his imagination.

It was a very happy and informal gathering and the retsina flowed like Grammatikakis's water.

Toward the end of the meal, and between excavations with a toothpick, Philippedes said, 'Yanni, tomorrow we have a big revelation for you! Tomorrow you will not go to Apikia by yourself. No! Tomorrow we *all* go to welcome to hour table there two desirable friends for you to surprise. Yes, Greek friends, yes, yes – from the village. And Metaxia will cook many many foods that you like too much. Yes.'

He paused and sucked his teeth in anticipation. 'Yes,' he continued, 'many foods: like houmus, like taramasalata, like dolmades, like, all these things. And to prepare these, as you might say, surprising eatables, we shall start very, very early in the morning with your bag, and you, now you know the path, will come later with your feet. And that I think is good, for then you will arrive with your stomach very alert. You agree?'

He awaited my acquiescence with his toothpick poised inquiringly. There was no argument: I adore surprising eatables and particularly dolmades. 'Bravo!' said Spiros, raising his glass, 'to tomorrow, Apikia, and the Hidden Paradise – Up My Bottom!'

Philippedes frowned. 'Spiros,' he said, 'for my opinion I think you must practise this er, toast phrase more carefully, yes – it is not Up *my* Bottom but Up *the* Bottom, yes. As Yanni informed us that is when you are drinking the liquids and emptying the glass and showing her bottom. Yes, yes that is correct Yanni, ne? Yes Spiros, you must practise practise practise to mend, as you might say, this hole in your memory.'

'But,' said Spiros belligerently, 'I – ' 'Tell me,' I said, coming quickly between father and son to prevent what promised to be an ugly domestic scene, 'the Hidden Paradise – is that the name of your cottage?' 'Yes,' said Spiros, 'it was because –' His father interrupted him. 'Forgive me Spiros, he said, 'I will inform Yanni, if you don't care. It was,' he continued, as Spiros left the room muttering and thinking darkly of the unfairness of parental authority, 'it was because of the Bible.'

'You know the Bible, Yanni,' he inquired tentatively and with the air of a man who had posed the question before and been dispirited by a negative reply, 'you know the Bible?'

'Yes,' I said, 'I do. Not intimately, but I know it.'

'Bravo!' said Philippedes, visibly relieved that on this occasion a lack of religious knowledge would not give the kiss of death to his story whilst still in its infancy, 'Bravo! And you are mindful then of the happenings of Adam and Heave?'

'Of course.'

'And the Eden Gardens?'

'I remember them well,' I said, hiding the thought that he made the region sound like an address in Palmers Green.

'Good,' said Philippedes, much encouraged by my familiarity with Genesis, 'Good! Splendid! For my opinion a beauteous story.'

'Indeed, yes.'

'Most beauteous.'

'I agree.'

'Exquarsite, as you might say.'

'Yes.'

'But,' said Philippedes, abruptly bringing the gloria to a close, 'all – pigs washings! Yes,' he continued, ignoring my glazed eyes, 'a beauteous story of pigs washings. Because for my opinion, Yanni, there are no talking snaks not nowhere never and morehever,' he advanced, warming to the subject, 'no mans who sleep as deep as to have unnoticed their ribs remov-ed in bed, as you might say. But,' he admitted, generously, 'still a beauteous, wondrous story.'

Temporarily drained of adjectives and ridding himself of the temptation to euhemerize on the one hand and eulogize on the other, he returned to the nub.

'Three years ago, Yanni,' he resumed, 'an English pair could not find no where to sleep in Andros so I made them welcome at the cottage for two days.'

He tapped twice upon the table emphasizing the time scale.

'Two *days*,' he repeated. 'But now, Yanni, I tell you something.'

Leaning toward me until our noses were in danger of marriage and enunciating slowly and dramatically in a lower key he said: 'Two *weeks* later they were still to arrive back in Hora!'

'Good Lord,' I said.

'Possibly!' said Philippedes, 'gooderlord! And why, you are asking silently in your head? I will inform you.'

At this juncture he glanced first over one shoulder, then the other as if suspecting the presence of invisible and unwelcome representatives of the popular Sunday Press, returned his nose to within an inch of mine and distilling each word, said: 'Because, Yanni, They Were Up To –' and here his eyes narrowed – 'THINGS.'

'Things?' I said, 'things?'

'Yes, Yanni,' he said, 'THINGS. They were, up-to-things. And I am knowing, Yanni, because I am hearing from many many peoples in the village who had been watchful through the vegetation, that all days long the pair was eating fruits from the trees – fruits like pomegranates and apples and other juiceful and powerful things, and running bare in the olives all the hours and not wanting to leave. They became, how to say, henergetic with each other. But when they left they was most relaxful – almost fatigu-ed as you might say.'

He stopped. Like Eskimos, our nostrils all but entwined.

'Katalavis, Yanni – you understand?'

'Katalava,' I said, 'I understand.'

'And so, Yanni,' concluded Philippedes, banging his palms on the table and straightening triumphantly – 'I am calling it the Hidden Paradise! And,' he added, 'who's better name you will say when you see it! But now let us go to the bed. Kali nichta, Yanni mu, kalinichta.'

As I undressed I thought about that conversation and marvelled at the Greeks' ability to make dramatic bricks from very little straw. And, I reflected, how strange that despite Andrew Marvell's reference to the 'nectarine and curious peach' I had been innocent of the aphrodisiac properties of soft fruit in general and the pomegranate in the particular. . . .

The next morning and long after the vanguard had left I set off brightly in their wake. Life, it seemed to me, was good once more and I was looking forward immensely to what the day promised to offer and especially to meeting their friends from Apikia; and those were the thoughts which occupied me as, with a song in my heart, I began the uphill trudge. Also I remember thinking how pleasant it was that at that time of the year I was probably the only foreign visitor in that part of Andros. Not that I do not love my countrymen – I do, dearly, but so often when I go abroad I do seem fated to encounter one or two fellow nationals from whom, without putting too fine a point upon it, I would hesitate to breed

I shall never know which of the gods on Olympus had taken exception to me that day nor why, but obviously one of them had done so, for as I neared the track leading downhill from the road to the Hidden Paradise, I saw two figures sitting on the stone parapet. One was very large, very red and male; the other was very angular, very white and, I conjectured, female.

The former, bareheaded and balding, was wearing a full sandy moustache, a tan sleeveless pullover, an orange short-sleeved Aertex shirt from the top of which gushed a neck scarf embroidered in the colours of the Royal Army Pay Corps and a pair of knee-length khaki shorts the like of which I had not seen since reading an illustrated book entitled *With Allenby in Palestine*. Save for a white floppy linen hat his companion's dress was nondescript. Instinctively I knew they were English, intuitively I knew how they would speak and indubitably I knew that I was on the threshold of a meeting with the Chairman of the Overseas Bores Committee and his wife. Also I harboured a horrid suspicion that we had met somewhere before. And I was right. At a distance of twenty paces my fears were realized when I heard him say:

'Ah yes! Yes! You see I wasn't wrong, Miggie! That's the feller all right – know him anywhere!'

His voice had the timbre of an expense account – Burgundy-rich, and heavy; its marriage to the flesh was perfect.

'Ah,' he bellowed, as the distance between us regrettably decreased, 'well, well, well, long time no see. Yes, I don't expect you remember me but my name's Prescott and this is my wife Margaret.' High-pitched and uncaring, and looking beyond my right shoulder, Margaret asked me how I did.

'Yes,' boomed Prescott, oblivious of the sudden drop in

The Prescotts

temperature, 'yes, we met at the Walters over at Frimley –
three years ago wasn't it, Miggie?' 'Two,' said Miggie, 'and
it was Bramley.' 'Yes, that's right,' said Prescott, 'three years
ago at Frimley. Yes, I remember I put Tiny Walter's back
right for her, didn't I, dear?' Miggie sniffed. 'Well not actually
right, dear, but you certainly made it better.' 'Yes,' said Prescott
unheedingly, 'right as rain! Well, well, well, what a small
world! And,' he added boisterously, 'what an extraordinary
coincidence you knowing the friends of our friends, what?'

His wife interrupted him with the precision of a laser beam:
'Well, they're not actually *friends*, do you see, because we've
only known them twenty-four hours but they put us up last
night and this afternoon they're taking us to the ferry so they
seem quite decent people really; but then one never knows
with foreigners does one?'

Prescott looked at her admiringly. 'Quite right,' he said,
'quite right – say no more! Say no more! Anyway,' he advised
me, 'we're on our way to Mycenae. Do you know Mycenae?
Very old, yes; and Dilys Powell's husband's buried there too,
yes. But to get back to our friends,' he continued, 'they said
they were lunching with your friends and I gather that your
friends said to our friends on the telephone this morning well –
you bring your friends along too because we've got an English
friend staying in the cottage and as he's walking here your
friends can meet him and he can show them the way. And then,
of course, he mentioned you by name and I said, Ah! So there
we are: funny people! Anyhow,' he concluded, untired by the
convoluted saga, 'lead on, Macduffoides.'

He shook with heavy appreciative laughter at his own
humour. 'Macduffoides!' he repeated. 'Not bad, what? – eh
Miggie? Not bad!'

Miggie looked at him coldly. 'It's lean on,' she said. 'I say,'
said Prescott, 'are you sure?' The frost turned to ice. 'Quite

sure,' she said. 'Oh well,' said Prescott unabashed, 'I expect you're right. I must say she's awfully good at that sort of thing you know, yes. Never had much time for the Bard myself, poetry's not my kind of country you know, never was – much preferred punting the old pill about, nothing like a good game of rugger, I always say – don't you agree? But anyway, old man, 'nuff said – we'll follow while you lean! What!' He roared with laughter again and smacked me on the back.

Praying silently that they might be turned to stone or not get worse I led the way to the cottage; but they did get worse. Much worse.

'Ah!' said Philippedes when we arrived, 'so you have met! Good! How nice for you, Yanni, to find companions of your kind this way, yes. Yes, another surprise for you, I think.' 'Yes,' I said, 'it was'; and introduced the Prescotts. 'I am,' said Philippedes, without the gift of foresight, 'most happy to meet you. And now, Yanni,' he said, piloting me toward his friends, 'I am most happy to introduce you to Arula and Demosthenes.'

'I say,' said Prescott, 'Demosthenes eh! What an extra-ordinary name – d'you hear that, Miggie – Demosthenes! Ha!' We shook hands.

'So!' said Philippedes beaming at everyone, 'now we are all happy I think, yes! We all understood some English and are desirous of the chat and of knowing, how to say, more phrases. But now I think we have some ouzo; and why not? Spiros – help hour guests!'

Miggie looked at her glass suspiciously. 'Is this the stuff which tastes like paraffin?' she asked.

'No,' said Prescott with equal indelicacy, 'that's retsina, the old retz. Yes I had a terrible time once with the retz – Harry Flakers for two days. Dreadful stuff, don't know how you chaps drink it! No,' he advised his wife inaccurately and unwisely, 'you drink this like schnapps. Go on Miggie, knock it back – put hair on yer chest!'

As one man the table arrested their glasses and looked first at him and then at her. Philippedes led the hunt. 'Put haar on –' and paused disbelievingly, 'her chest? Your wife's chest has the ha –'

'I'd like to see your garden,' said Miggie shrilly and with more than a hint of desperation, 'your garden – I'd like to see it!'

Philippedes was superb – the perfect host. 'Of course,' he said, 'and why not? And you too, Yanni, I think, yes. Come!'

'Good oh,' said Prescott; and drained his glass.

Justifiably Philippedes was very proud of his gardens and he spared no pains to go into detail as he gave us a conducted tour of the terraced slopes, and half an hour later and on our return journey his enthusiasm was still waxing. 'Yes,' he said, as we clambered upward toward the house, 'all is very, very beauteous here. Here we have all things for, as you might say, the eyes, the nose and the belly. Yes, for hexample over there as you can see are many many grapps, very good grapps and –'

'Ah yes,' said Prescott, 'so there are. Yes, we've got jolly good grapes in Guildford, haven't we, Miggie?'

'Yes: we have a vinery you know.'

'Really? How nice, yes. And over here there are many many oranges.'

'Yes, are they seedless? Ours are, aren't they, dear?'

'Yes, we have an orangery you know.'

'Oh! Really? How – er, nice; yes, nice. And you can see also the roses bush, many, many roses bush and –'

'Ah, yes. Yes, we pride ourselves on our roses, don't we, Miggie?'

'Yes, we have a rosa –' She drew back from the precipice in

the nick of time. 'Pogs,' she said sharply, 'mind your Pringle on the prickles.'

Philippedes stopped in his tracks and looked perplexed. 'Pringle?' he inquired, 'Pringle? What is this, the Pringle?'

'Ah,' said Prescott, 'that's a jolly good question that, isn't it, Miggie? Bit difficult to explain though really. It's er –'

'Perhaps,' said Philippedes, trying to help him out, 'it is a part of the body, a very, as you might say, careful part of the body?'

'No, no, no,' said Prescott hurriedly, 'no, no, no, nothing like that at all. Really these chaps,' he said turning to me, 'one track minds, haven't they? No,' he resumed, 'it's a sort of trade name, a very famous name for a very famous, er, clorth.'

'Well not a clorth exactly,' said Miggie, 'it's a very famous name for a jumpah, a woollen jumpah – a name given to something very, very good made of wool.'

'Ah!' said Philippedes, his eyes bright with enlightenment, 'now I understood – a Woolwarths!'

Miggie looked at him. 'Not in the least,' she said. 'A Pringle, is a knitted Rolls Royce.'

'I think we return,' said Philippedes.

We sat down to a laden table on the verandah and lunched marvellously under a living canopy of vine leaves, and it was there that Prescott reached his peak of frightfulness: we were treated to a ball-by-ball commentary on our hosts' eating habits as if they were absent.

'Well! well! well! I see! So we all dig in together do we? Well! well! well! Do you notice Miggie, how they all use the same bowl – do you notice that? Touch of the old communals, eh? Still when in Rome, what? All right, dear – Greece. Still, I suppose you all go and have a shower after this – wash the old shirt out, eh? Do the old dhobi, what? Ha! ha! Oh, I say! Oh, my dear feller, you are a dirty boy, aren't you! Dear, oh dear!

I say did you see that, Miggie? All down his – Ha! ha! ha! Still they don't seem to mind, do they? Just like the Turks, eh?'

His voice grew louder and louder and his eyes more pink with every glass.

I sat there deeply embarrassed. And then, just as I was contemplating strangulation as a means to ending his commentary, providence intervened in the shape of Philippedes's son. Leaving his chair at the end of the table and facing his father's guest squarely, he raised his glass in salutation and said: 'And now I say something to you in English – Up your bottom!'

They left very shortly afterwards, their features working horribly. To this day I do not know if they reached Mycenae or not. Nor do I care. But when Spiros came to England later in the year I lavished attention upon him.

Just before the Philippedes departed en famille, John Philippedes put his hand on Spiro's shoulder and turned to me. 'Yanni,' he said, 'I am very proud of my son this night!'

'Yanni,' I said, 'you have every reason to be. He has the makings of a great man!'

Spiros looked at me and winked. 'Bottoms up,' he said, 'bottoms up.' He was no fool.

When they had gone I sat on the verandah and twiddled the dials of the transistor they had left behind. From somewhere in Europe came the strains of Beethoven's Ninth Symphony and as Schiller's Ode grew in majesty so the night wind sighed gently through the sky and cut a path across the distant Aegean. It was very peaceful.

CHAPTER IV

Lessons and Lamentations

I HAD A SHORT night – not because of insomnia but because a Grecian day is too precious to waste between the sheets, and so, just before six o'clock, I got up, sat on a slope behind the cottage and listened to Apikia coming to life. Owls hooted their last farewells, mules brayed their first good mornings and five roosters competed for which could welcome the sun more stridently. And with its coming the insect choir tuned up and grew stronger by the minute.

Later, and after a breakfast of yoghurt and honey, innumerable cups of coffee and a one-sided conversation with some hens of dubious origin who had looked in to see if there were any pickings to be had, I lit my first pipe of the day and strolled down from the stone-flagged and vine-covered verandah to the first terrace and looked back to take a detailed stock of my surroundings.

Philippedes's appreciation of the Hidden Paradise was well founded: it deserved the title. The cottage, white plastered and old, two up, two down with a tenuous external addition of a lizard-patrolled lavatory in which one was never without company, snuggled in the lee of the Kuwara mountains. Its flat roof anxiously bore the weight of an enormous, and as I was to discover, inefficient galvanized water tank which was reached by means of a rusty and rickety iron ladder with missing rungs. It contained a senile and unco-operative ball-cock and my daily meetings with it are the only unpleasant memories I have of my stay: we grew to hate each other.

At the back of the cottage, and higher on the slopes, was the village of Apikia from where the waters of the Sarisa Springs flowed and fed in turn a rocky stream which gurgled and trickled through the grounds on its way to the sea. Turning my back on the house I looked over small orchards of fruit trees, across a valley and on to the blue waters of the Aegean. Thickly planted windbreaks of cypress trees flanked the left of my picture, and high to my right I could see the road to Apikia running like a white ribbon against the hills.

As I stood there drinking in the scenery and listening to the end-of-season humming of bees from Philippedes's hives a goat picked its way down from the verandah. It halted when it saw me and bleated uncertainly. It was followed by a ver-minous-looking old gentleman wearing spectacles and carrying a stick.

'Yasas!' I said. He returned the greeting. 'Hallo folks,' he said, and hit the goat a resounding blow on its backside. 'Yes, folks,' he said, continuing to address me in the plural as it flew past me, 'Noo you was here. Yes siree!'

He anticipated my question. 'Lived in Pittsburgh for thirty years. Had a diner there. Made a heap, folks, made a heap. You know the States, folks?' We nodded. 'Good place, folks,' he said. 'Staying long?' he asked. I shook my head. 'A few days,' I said.

'By yourself?'

I nodded.

He laughed bronchially. 'Last guy wasn't,' he said. 'No

siree, he wasn't. Stayed a fortnight. With a girl. Watched them every day. Gee,' he said, 'did they have a ball. At it the –'

'I know,' I said, hurriedly interrupting him, 'Philippedes told me.'

He looked at me disappointedly. 'Oh,' he said, 'he did, huh?' And changed the subject. 'Tried the water yet – the spring water?'

'Not yet,' I said.

'Well,' he said ,'they say it's real good for the di-gestion, real good. But me, folks? I don't rate it too much: it makes me fart. So long, folks – see you around.' And with that sobering thought he left me.

Happily the spring water did not have that effect on me. I spent four blissful days in the Hidden Paradise, and despite the absence of temptation with which the energetic latter-day Adam and Eve had been blessed three years before, hourly I became more understanding of their disinclination to leave the site. There is a good deal to be said for an envrionment where, without moving from the horizontal, one can pluck a grape from overhanging vines and feed at will. I revelled in the situation. Not that I employed myself solely in this manner; nor could I. Fond as I am of fruit there are limits to the quantity I can eat with impunity, and as there was no refrigeration in the cottage I had to replenish my stocks of other foods day by day.

Each day I walked the four hundred yards of the rock-strewn track which switchbacked and zigzagged to a stone bridge, yellow and green with moss and lichen, and spanning a gorge, clambered up roughly hewn steps, each set one foot above the other and with a gradient encouraging cardiac fatigue, reached the main road and panted up hill to the village to do my shopping and to exercise my Greek.

From a purchasing point of view it was not a particularly demanding operation – one was not faced with the decision about where to stop. There were only two stores theoretically vying for custom, and as one of these bore an undated notice written in faded ink advising me that the proprietor had gone to America but would be back shortly, from necessity I was directed to the other establishment whose incumbent was unaffected by wanderlust. This was a remarkable place and reminded me very much of Tenniel's illustration of the dream, sheep-owned shop in 'Alice Through the Looking Glass'. It was small, dark, incredibly smelly, and held everything for the hungry or afflicted.

The doyen of this embryonic Fortnum and Mason was a small lady dressed entirely in black. Whether she affected this garb to advertise a prolonged period of mourning or because of a chameleon-like desire to match the general decor I never discovered, but her first appearance from the shadows made me jump violently. My second reaction when her features grew plainer was that she was Methuselah's sister; and as I recovered from my initial fright and my eyes became dark accustomed, it seemed to me that much of her stock was of a similar age. This she displayed with a cavalier disregard for the finer points of merchandising.

Glass-covered refrigerated fish gaped glassy-eyed in frosty disbelief at near-by wilting and perspiring cheeses; condensed milk cohabited unhappily with metal polishes and yoghurt; tinned luncheon meats of dubious condition ominously shared shelves with panaceas for flatulence and oral hygiene preparations; there were oils for cooking, oils for lighting, oils for sewing machines and the relief of constipation, jars of sweetmeats, sacks of spices, antidotes for rust and piles, shampoos, soaps and washing powders and, praise be, row upon row of coffee essence each bearing the inscription CAMP and a picture of Lord Kitchener standing in front of a tent. It was a brand I had not seen since my very early childhood and I gazed upon the bottled ranks with reverence.

Mrs Methuselah also sold what euphemistically was known as bread. She baked this herself in an antique oven and it was assured of a ready market: the Greeks enjoy bread. They consume vast quantities of it and wisely eat it as soon as possible and as quickly as possible after its emergence from the bakery, a luxury which either by design or coincidence I was not allowed to enjoy during my stay in Apikia; and to my detriment. The Cycladean loaf does not weather well.

I cannot say why because I am ignorant of the more intimate details of panification on Andros, but what I do know is that there is something in its character which prevents it from ageing gracefully – it becomes careworn and brutalized within hours of its birth, a harshness comes upon it. No, Andros bread must be eaten within a maximum of eight hours or not at all. After that only the masochistic, the very hungry or the insane will take it on, and I saw overwhelming evidence in support of my theory in the faces of the island's elderly who, with advancing years, had become less prudent: there were gaps among the dental tombstones – sometimes quite large gaps, and I drew my own conclusion. Not that the superannuated were dismayed or deterred by their losses – far from it.

One of the kindest, most cultured septuagenarians I was to meet on the island belonged to this use-what-you-have-and-be-thankful school. His name was Demosthenes and he possessed six teeth. Unfortunately for him, and everyone else within range, all but one were on the same side of his face, but he coped extraordinarily well really. He reminded me of an old tom-cat of mine who, with his face an inch from the plate would move it from right to left in short staccato movements along whatever he was eating and then, when his head was over his left shoulder, he would pause, gulp, and then go cross-eyed as the offering went down. Demosthenes's action was very like that; but he was a dear man. And a talented one. He played the violin badly and chess superbly, he drank deeply of life and his whisky from the cask, wrote revolutionary poetry in the small hours and read it long and aloud and alone at noon; and he painted and he sketched; but above all, he was the only person I have ever met who could coax music from a cooked crayfish. He could make it sing.

His technique was unsophisticated. Favouring the two-handed approach, with the half shell clutched at both ends and held just below eye-level, its appendages pointing in all directions like wayward radio antennae homing for a wavelength, he attacked it with all the panache of a demented bagpipe player. Somehow, in his hands, it seemed to come alive. And when at one stage in the pibroch it slipped from his grasp and leapt into my lap I was sure that it had; but within seven minutes not a claw nor feeler remained unexplored, unplayed, unsucked nor blown through. It was a remarkable performance and I can still hear the sounds and sense his enthusiasm.

Many of the dentally bereft attempt to emulate Demosthenes but none can match his virtuosity. He is the Master: but all share his philosophy with regard to their common handicap. Without exception none mourn their fallen molars nor grieve for their lost incisors – rather they lavish love and attention upon the survivors. Exquisitely decorated within, and regardless of expense, the mouths of Old Andros glitter with all the treasure of Hephaestus's workshop, and with my hand on my heart I cannot recall seeing so much gold since I looked down a mine in the Transvaal.

I did not search particularly for these revelations, nor was there any need – they presented themselves readily during everyday conversation. No doubt many Britons have similar

His technique was unsophisticated

built-in reserves of wealth but one is seldom afforded the opportunity of seeing them.

When an Englishman extends a greeting, be it, 'Good morning', 'Hallo' or even when he uses the transatlantic importation 'Hi', depending on his social class he will deliver the salutation either through the nose or allow it to escape unwillingly from the side of his mouth; but whichever mode is employed his lips will remain closed. Not so the Greeks: 'Ya!' they will say from the pits of their stomachs and their mouths wide open, 'Ya!' And one is afforded a splendid opportunity of observing Greek dentistry.

'Ya' was one of the first words I learned in Greece. It is a diminutive of 'Yasu' or 'Yasas' and means 'Blessings'. And it can also be translated as the equivalent of 'Wotcher!' It may be used at any hour of the day and plainly is less formal than 'Kalimera' and 'Kalispera' which are 'Good morning' and 'Good evening' respectively. And there is also 'Herete' – 'Greetings' – that, too, is timeless although in some quarters it is considered proper only if used in the afternoon.

It took me some time to digest these and other finer points of language and etiquette during my early days in the islands. There was much to learn and I did it the hard way. There can be few people who, radiating bonhomie, have sailed into a crowded grocer's shop and greeted a disbelieving assembly with 'Squid! everybody, Squid!' The words Kalimera and calamaris are not dissimilar to the untutored ear . . . for some while after that episode I was known as Yanni the Squid. The indigenous population also took some time to recover. However, I persevered.

Unlike my father who, when abroad, only opened his mouth to admit food and looked upon all foreigners with deep suspicion, I was anxious to establish a rapport with them and to do this with any degree of success in darkest Greece one must have at least a nodding acquaintance with the modern tongue. Ancient Greek is of little use – that I possessed, but while the ability to state precisely what it was that Agamemnon said to Clytemnestra before she put the boot in has its uses, that particular talent does not get one very far in the field of communication. And so during my short stay in the tiny village of Apikia I continued my linguistic struggles daily, with Mrs Methuselah's establishment as the main seat of learning.

I listened and watched; and I learned what no phrasebook can tell one – the importance of the gesture. I am not denigrating the phrasebook because although most seem to be designed for use by the ultimate in misfortune – 'I have trodden on a sea urchin', 'I have been bitten by a dog', 'I have been stung by a jellyfish', 'I am suffering from my . . .' and here the space is left blank for the martyr's choice, some of them do give additional marginal information about certain words. 'The word "oche" meaning "no",' advises one publication, 'is often accompanied by an upward tilting of the face or a momentary raising of the eyebrows together with a click of the tongue. This gesture may altogether replace the word and often puzzles the uninitiated.'

This is quite true. However, what the booklet does not say is that apart from implying the negative, the same mannerism can also mean 'I have a foreign body lodged in the back of my throat but I shall be quite all right once I have gone "haach"!' But this is a cavil. Of far greater importance is the omission of any reference to the gesture employed when saying 'Ya!'

'Ya!' is delivered, not only with verve, but with the hand raised to eye level – always the hand comes up in salutation. This was one of the first things I noticed in Apikia – the friendly gesture. And as there was nothing I wished more than to be friendly, in the Greek manner, I Yasas-ed and Ya-ed and gestured with equal abandon.

On the whole, people seemed to be quite pleased. Most of them smiled and returned the compliment: some even asked me if I was in good health. Admittedly one or two seemed a little withdrawn and just muttered but I was never actually rejected; that is until my very last day.

It was a Sunday: early in the morning and as I was breakfasting on the verandah of the Hidden Paradise, Philippedes materialized out of the vines like an equine wraith.

'Yasas, Yanni,' he said as we embraced, 'Yasas, Yasas – ti kanite?'

'Kala,' I said.

'Bravo,' he said, and sat down. 'And that,' he said, 'is enough of the Greek – now for the English I should say, and why not? Yanni,' he said, foraging among the mixed fruits, 'I am happy for you! I have a pension for you! Yes, a good pension! In Niborio! It is the house of a builder man – almost in the sea as you might say, with the bed, very very good the bed, the working shower – the *working* shower, Yanni,' he emphasized, 'and also,' he added through a mouthful of fig, 'also the towel! So, Yanni,' he continued, defigging his fingers individually by suction, 'you can have the dips the one minute and using the toilet the next within metres! And that is good I think, yes?'

'Yanni,' I said, 'it sounds splendid.'

'Yes,' said Philippedes, adding an additional stain to the already taxed table cloth, 'for my opinion it *is* splendid, and more hover, Yanni, you can occupy it now if you desire. Together we can go now or, if you desire, we can go personally. Yes, I with your baggage in the car once she is all right – so much steam, Yanni, so much steam – I am not able properly to see the road on the way hup – there is I think an absence of water somewhere, yes I think so, and you with your feet later but,' he concluded, 'it is up to me.'

I hope I did not appear uncharitable but as I still had memories of the car ride with Philippedes from Gavrion, when his radiator was in good working order, I elected to go on foot and to meet him later at his flat in Hora. And so fig-filled and laden, Philippedes departed and late in the afternoon I turned my back on Apikia and started the long downhill walk to the coast. The day was still glorious with the sun midway to the horizon in a cloudless sky and I walked briskly without a care in the world nor a soul in sight. Lizards scuttled into the privacy of rocks as I disturbed their roadside siestas, but it was not until I had covered half the distance that I saw other travellers.

Suddenly, and about three hundred yards ahead of me, a very tired mule appeared from around one of the hairpin bends of the road. As the distance closed between us I could see that it was bearing, and- with fortitude, one of Andros's more senior citizens back to his village after a day on the ouzo.

It is never easy to judge the age of the Greek peasantry, but at a rough estimate the collarless but stripe-shirted passenger topped by a flat cap and draped in a shapeless black jacket with matching trousers was in his early sixties, but afflicted with premature senility; and his steed appeared to be in a similar condition. Obviously, it had been a very good Sabbath for the rider, if a somewhat tedious one for the latter, for there sat a six-bottle man if ever I saw one. He was huddled over his mangy mount like a happy sack of potatoes, clearly feeling very little pain, and as we neared each other I could hear that he was singing, or rather intoning, a plaintive little song. It was one which I had heard Spiros sing some days before and was all about love and friendship and how beautiful everything is, and I thought how good it was to see somebody so at peace with the world; my heart warmed to him.

'Ya!' I bellowed as we came to within hailing distance and I could see the white of his moustache and the red of his eyes, 'Ya!' And flung up my hand.

Mercifully time has blurred much of the disagreeable detail of what followed; but not all. Abruptly the song about love and friendship died on his lips which drew back most unpleasantly from his gums as he jerked into an upright position, and then, with an agility belying both his years and his condition, he propelled himself from the saddle, staggered toward me like a novice on ice, and seized me by the shirt. 'Uurrgh-urh-urh!' he said, shaking me like a rag doll, 'Uurrgh-urh-urh!' he repeated, as buttons flew in all directions, and for a full minute demonstrated the power of Greek rhetoric, which he ended with a final 'Uurgh' and a well-aimed spit on my left boot. Then walking backwards like an erratic slow-motion film in reverse and shaking both fists at me he remounted with his face still contorted and puce with anger.

That I had ruined his Sunday was obvious, and as I gazed after their retreating figures and heard his continued invective growing fainter the mule made it abundantly plain that it too had been upset by the turn of events; but they are nervous animals at the best of times and one must be grateful that they cannot fly. What was less evident was how I had distressed them and it was this thought which preoccupied me for the rest of my journey to Niborio. No one enjoys upsetting people, and I was subdued when later I made my pre-arranged meeting with Philippedes.

'Yanni,' said Philippedes, after we had seated ourselves in long chairs and the retsina had frosted our glasses, 'something, I know, is wrong, is – inharmoonious. You are, how to say, down in the lips. Also your shirt is in splits – what the matter is?'

He listened attentively and without interruption to my resumé.

'Yanni,' he said, draining his glass and replenishing it, 'Yanni – thenkatalava! I do not understand. This is, for my opinion most strange, yes. Perhaps it is that this peasant fellow has too much trouble with the bottles – ne?'

'Ne,' I said, 'Yes. Perhaps.'

'But,' said Philippedes, expelling an unwanted olive stone through the open window and toward the dying sun, 'repeat to me again, Yanni, more carefully what it was you did.'

'Well,' I said, lighting my pipe, 'all I did was to say "Ya" – and wave at him. Like this,' I said; and demonstrated for him.

A fine spray of retsina covered me as Philippedes exploded into his glass, and was overcome with a paroxysm of coughing.

'Oh, my God!' he said, his eyes bulging alarmingly, 'Oh, my God! Now I . . .' He stopped for running repairs.

'Yanni,' he said, mopping his eyes and forehead, 'allow me to tell you a small small lesson. "Ya" is fine. "Yasas" is fine and wavings is fine but, Yanni, never, nowhere, no how when you are raising the hand to do it with her five fingers hopen because that, Yanni, is how to say,' and he paused, 'giving the two fingers?'

He leaned toward me. 'You know, Yanni, the two fingers?'

I nodded, 'Yes,' I said, 'I know the two fingers.' And started to perspire freely.

'There is a small word for the two fingers – ne?'

'Ne.'

'I cannot find it in my lexicon.'

'No.'

'I have looked through many pages for this small word.'

'Yes.'

'But it avoids me.'

'It would.'

'But I think it is, how to say, meaning – go away violently with filth.'

'Well –'

'Or go away with much coarseness?'

'Er – well, yes. Yes.'

'So you are saying to him, Blessings – and go away violently with much coarseness and filth! But do not mind, Yanni,' said Philippedes bringing the tutorial to a close, 'do not mind! Avrio, tomorrow, after the hypnos the – er, the sleeps, he will not remember the fingers so do not have the worry.'

But I did have the worry. Suddenly, and like a drowning man recalling his past, I remembered vividly the sharp intake of breath of Mrs Methuselah at the cheese counter when I greeted her on the Wednesday. At the time, and with the comfort of innocence, I had attributed her reaction to the inhalation of old stock: but, above all, I understood only too clearly why the benign smile on the face of the local priest had frozen stiff that morning. But it is an ill wind . . .

After Philippedes had guided me down to my pension in Niborio but before we bade each other goodnight, he said: 'Yanni – please! One thing before you are put to rest. Inform me please – what is the phrase of the two fingers?'

I informed him.

'Ah, yes,' he said, writing it down in pencil on the back of an envelope addressed to the National Bank of Greece, 'yes, yes, that is the small word. I remember now. It was Andrei Eugenides who told me. Andrei Eugenides,' he repeated. 'He is a good man but, how to say, full of filth; you will like him very much I think. Ke tora philimu, kalinichta – and sweet sleeps.'

Homer might not have approved but that is how Philippedes improves upon his colloquial vocabulary; and as he volunteered the Greek equivalent to me, how I added to mine.

I did enjoy the sweet sleeps that night but the sandman did not come immediately. For some time I remained awake, and with my hands behind my head, looked at the ceiling, pondering on the possible outcome should Philippedes forget to erase his memorandum on the envelope.

CHAPTER V

Tittle-tattle and Tavernas

PHILIPPEDES'S FLAT WAS in the capital of Andros – Hora. It is a small, brilliant white town built on a steep peninsula and traffic is forbidden in its centre. It has two tree-lined squares, one main street, a maze of others, and an aura of bourgeois respectability: Hora has a club.

Below the township, and reached by steep wide Buchan flights of steps, lies the village of Niborio. It skirts the sickle of the bay and at high tide no more than a dozen dusty yards separate the buildings from the water's edge on the right.

All creatures, great and small, use the steps of Hora. Men and women, young and old, goats and mules and cats and dogs, suckling pigs and scrawny hens, all pick their ways up and down the shallow treads breaking their journeys to shop or peer in the tiny stores and larger shops on either side.

At the lower levels, where the steps give out, there is a narrow sunless street with shops and tavernas with dim interiors, and in their shadows the old men sit, talking and sipping, engrossed in tablis, cards and gossip. Eventually the buildings on the right fall away, the sea comes into view again and once more the glare narrows the eyes. An open stretch of road runs the length of the beach until it joins the route to Apikia. On the left is a petrol station with a single pump, a bicycle store and a lump of buildings in a cluster and then the dwelling houses of Niborio. And it was among those that Philippedes had found me my pension.

The name of the owner was Katsiotis. A man of few words and a builder by trade, he was a walking advertisement for the industry. His person was decorated liberally with the hallmarks of his occupation and he moved slowly in an omnipresent grey blanket of dust. When he stopped to cough, which he did frequently, the ensuing cloud gave him the appearance of Marley's ghost. I well remember how, after one particularly violent attack, he disappeared completely.

It was difficult to know what Katsiotis was thinking. No doubt if you pricked him he would bleed; if you wronged him assuredly he would seek revenge. Beyond question he was as emotional as any Jew, Gentile or Greek, but as his features were set firm in a permanent layer of cement which rendered him utterly incapable of facial expression he remained an enigma to me for the whole of my stay. Not that I saw much of him, but our initial meeting made an impression upon me.

The previous evening, following Philippedes's introduction and departure, he guided me up a flight of external steps, under an archway, turned left through an open door and halted before a large refrigerator which vibrated and hummed with inefficiency. 'Fridge,' he said, parting his plastered lips with difficulty, and opened the door. Some tired chicken livers flopped out on to the floor. Katsiotis gazed at them un-emotionally for a moment and then returned them to their roosting place in silence and garnished with a paprika of brick dust. 'Fridge,' he repeated, imprisoning them again, and led me into a corridor.

We halted. Stiffly Katsiotis pointed to a closed cubicle to his right. 'Washings,' he indicated, dispensing more building material as he raised his arm, 'washings. And here,' and he opened an opposite door, 'is beds.' We entered.

It was a large, cool, terrazzo-floored room with white walls and furnished with a wardrobe, a washbasin and two beds.

'Endaxi?' inquired Katsiotis, 'Okkay?' Quickly I took in the surroundings. Apart from where his foot prints had blazed a trail the room was spotlessly clean.

'Endaxi,' I said.

Katsiotis grunted, moved toward the door, and then turned, his hand upon the handle. 'You will,' he said, forcing the words out in a cement-laden voice, 'be using only the one bed?'

I nodded. 'Endaxi,' said Katsiotis. He gave me a long look. 'Endaxi,' he repeated. And left.

To this day I am uncertain why he posed the question, but at the time it aroused uneasy feelings in me that he was remembering the actions of a previous single occupant who had not only rung the changes between the two resting places, but also committed enormities on alternate nights. I was not at peace until I had made a thorough investigation and discovered no malpractice. What my search did reveal, however, was the construction of the beds.

Under the mattresses were planks – four to be precise – and spaced at eight-inch intervals. It was an invaluable find. After a brief but traumatic trial period upon one bed I removed the timbers from the other, added them to the frame of mine and no longer felt that I was lying upon an inverted seed box. But on the whole it was a good pension. Moreover, it was one in which I was afforded a rare opportunity of studying the behavioural patterns of other visiting nationals.

Prior to my visit to Andros and excluding a short but tempestuous relationship with a girl named Magda – I was eleven at the time – my knowledge of the Hungarian people was negligible. I knew they were Magyar and moody, inclined to rebellion and rhapsodies and their nation had produced Molnar and Bartok. As a small boy I was told the story of how one of them, Kossuth by name, had kept a shoe-box full of Hungarian earth under his bed when in exile. This I was advised was patriotism: to me it suggested that he had kept a cat as a companion, and I said so – unwisely. Later in life I came to know and to share their liking for vintage Tokay, but until my sojourn at Pension Katsiotis I had no idea of their insatiable desire for fresh water.

There were seven Hungarians staying in that pension. And there was one shower. Sharing it with them was an experience which I shall always remember with clarity but without pleasure.

By Greek standards, Katsiotis's shower was unique – it worked. The Hungarian contingent recognized the novelty with enthusiasm. They were never out of it. To them it was not only a place for lavation but a shrine – they all but slept in it and I am sure that when they went home and people asked: 'Did you have a good time in Greece?' they chorused, 'Yes! the shower was magnificent.'

They were obsessed with it. No matter what hour of the day it was, whenever I presented myself for ablution they were in residence – never in single occupation but en masse; like an aquatic goulash. Hour after hour I would hear them as pathetically I clutched my bar of Lifebuoy and waited for the break which never came. Shrieks and slaps and bursts of the Radetsky March delivered by a foam-encrusted tenor fell on my unwashed ears. It was like sauna with song.

They never spoke to me. As they emerged through the steam, but always leaving one of their number behind, presumably to guard the soap until the next wave took over, they would merely look, nod curtly, blow a soap bubble or two and then drip their betowelled way to their rooms. For some while I was convinced they were spies, and it came as something of an anticlimax when I discovered that they were technicians from the local power station doing their laundry.

I came to know them quite well. They were, I reflected as I lathered myself in the small hours and listened to their snores, really very nice and, I reminded myself, one must give and take in life.

The pension was well situated in the village. Each morning I would leave it and, turning to my right, walk the four hundred yards or so to the long narrow street where the sun never shone – the old ones' road I called it – and breakfast at Leonardo's.

Dear Leonardo. He was, and I hope still is, the owner of a taverna which like himself was small, dark and very old and in need of fumigation. It had what house agents would describe as a 'lived-in look'. To the right of the room, and perpendicular to the once cream wall, two wooden tables with blue-checked multi-stained plastic coverings and uneven legs stood precariously, with equally unstable wicker-seated chairs, upon a blue and white tiled diamond-patterned floor. Two more tables in similar condition and decor abutted the opposite wall, a fifth occupied the centre, and chairs filled the remaining spaces.

To the rear was a glass-fronted rectangular display cabinet. What mysteries were housed therein was difficult to determine through the patina, but the PVC top was decorated with a vase of artificial roses, sundry bottles containing near-lethal distillations of Leonardo's own making, and the fuscous corpses of several half-smoked and forgotten cigarettes.

Behind, and under the triangle of a zinc cooker hood of monstrous proportions, stood a two-ringed stove fuelled by butane. When ignited this produced some of the finest un-controlled pyrotechnics I have ever seen.

Mural decorations were many and varied; Leonardo's artistic taste was catholic if undiscriminating. A young woman bearing a striking resemblance to the Mona Lisa, but holding a cigarette, slanted a Gioconda smile through its rising smoke toward another female addict favouring a Cleopatra hairstyle and a rival brand; there was a nineteenth-century gentleman complete with fowling piece and an improbably large pile of dead pigeons; a large sepia photograph of an elderly lady dressed in black for whom, one judged, nothing had gone right since puberty; and a coloured diagram in reds and yellows featuring two hermaphrodites demonstrating cardiac resuscitation in ten easy stages. Over this domain ruled Leonardo.

Cloth-capped, brown-eyed and moustachioed, gold-toothed and black-nailed, wrinkled and unshaven and wearing an expression of benign villainy, his appearance was that of a fully paid-up member of the Mafia. He walked stiff-legged and stooped, his arms hanging, motionless, and with open-fingered hands . . . imaginary pistols waited to be drawn. I was told that he had been quite a terror in his youth. He was, in fact, a retired muleteer.

A good deal of his time was devoted to the making of raki (a particularly vicious spirit which is downed in one gulp like schnapps) and much more to the tasting of it. One horrid day he introduced me to this devil's brew. At breakfast. Standing over at my table he pointed to the thick small glass he was holding.

'Raki,' he said reverently, and with a mental genuflection, 'raki!' I nodded and laughed nervously. 'Yes,' I said, 'raki.' And my mouth became dry. I had heard stories of Leonardo's raki and had no wish for it, particularly with fried eggs. But there was no escape.

'Drink,' said Leonardo, in much the same tone as the bearer

of hemlock must have used to Socrates, 'drink!' It was the only word of English he knew and it rang like a death knell. I had a moment of silent prayer, then, rising from the table I did the only decent thing – I drank up for England. Two seconds later I fell down for England.

When I recovered my sight, the first thing that came into focus was the resuscitation poster. As it ebbed and flowed and swam before me and the androgynous ones leapt from section to section, the reason for its inclusion in the art gallery became clear. And as Leonardo assisted me to a chair, dimly I recalled the maxim about bewaring the Greeks when they arrived with gifts. But his eggs were superb, and on all the other raki-free mornings I enjoyed them hugely. Products of the free-range system, they were large and brown and always appeared on a tin plate, fried in oil. I did make one attempt to instruct him in the art of poaching his hen-fruit but my efforts came to nought. He was a conservative man by nature and one who disliked change of any kind – eleven days after our first meeting he was still wearing the same shirt; and after a fortnight the same fly was still stiff and supine in my ashtray. The Greeks, I noticed, do have a great reverence for death.

But no fly had ever settled upon Leonardo. He did not allow life to pass him by, he was a keen observer of it and, I concluded, no mean impresario.

The first day I breakfasted alone, but I felt Leonardo eyeing me like a hawk from the dim shadows behind his bar. He was, I sensed, making mental notes. 'This man,' I could hear him saying privately, 'has style – a different technique from me – he does not engulf his eggs in one but piece by piece – truly he is worth watching.' And I am sure I was correct.

On the second day I had a spectator. Within five minutes of my arrival an elderly, grey-faced man appeared. He glanced quickly in my direction, and nodded knowingly to Leonardo.

Then, straddling a chair and resting his arms upon its back and his chin upon his arms and ordering neither food nor drink, he stared at me, unblinkingly.

I started to make mistakes – things went down the wrong way, portions of white ricocheted off the table, yellow went on my shirt – Nanny would have been livid. I wished he would leave. Eventually he did; and returned the following day with three of his old school chums. On the fourth day all the ringside seats were taken. By the fifth an assembly of eight were gathered to watch The Englishman Eat His Eggs, and at the end of the week I almost got a round of applause before I broke the yolks. Leonardo, I was convinced, was charging them a drachma a head.

They were a strange audience. Mutely, they sat in a semicircle watching me through their cigarette smoke in keen and appreciative silence; but despite their consuming interest in my egg and oil routine they were not rude. Without exception all of them had a natural courtesy – these were Nature's Gentlemen, unspoiled by our pace of life. Unhurriedly they would make the six-yard pilgrimage from one side of the road to the other, from one taverna to Leonardo's; without pressure they would drink their ouzo and worry away an hour with their beads and then, content with my cabaret, they would retrace their steps, all the way back to the other side of the street. As someone has said there is a Greek word equivalent to the Spanish 'mañana' but somehow it lacks the same sense of urgency.

They were wonderful characters, those ancients of Niborio. They epitomized the spirit of that part of the island where even the waves found it an effort to get up the beach. There nothing moved quickly except perhaps the lizards with whom I shared my lunch of cheese and apple in a little cove where I used to bask in the sun with them. With the blue sky above me, the sand between my toes and a blue-black rock at my back, idly I would toss an offering toward them as they waited and watched, like statues, between cracks in the rocks. Then, green and grey, spasmodically they would dart toward the core or rind with movements of arrested shock. But even they gave up the ghost after their first tongue-flickering efforts and would lie motionless, only a pulse beat showing they were alive, and watch me through cheese-dulled eyes, like the patrons of Leonardo's taverna: they had much in common with them. And so did the cats of Hora.

Just as television aerials are part of the scenery of our English town or city, so cats are part of the scene of Hora and Niborio – never have I seen so many. There were hundreds – thousands of them. Black cats, grey cats, white cats, ginger cats, tortoise-shell and marmalade, spotted or with stripes, cats with three legs and one eye, cats with tails and cats without, fat cats, thin cats, dirty cats and clean cats, battle-scarred mousers past their prime, middle-aged mothers heavy with kitten, nubile young ones raring to go – all types and conditions were represented.

Wherever I went there was a cat. Shy ones, squinting with anxiety, peeped at me from around corners or over walls, polite ones passed the time of day with me, and rude ones put out their tongues and ran away; but mostly they were to be seen snoring their heads off and dreaming either of the joys of the previous evening or the delights of the night to come; for the night is when they come alive. That is when the adrenalin starts to flow, when every able-bodied tom under ninety feels ichor in his veins and imagines that he is Zeus incarnate. But the next morning you see them . . . undeified and spent, staggering through the alleyways with glassy expressions as they look for a place to recover but not, alas, before they've sung their sagas to the fading stars and told the story of their deeds in true Homeric style.

It is not Macbeth who murders sleep on Andros but the Grecian toms of Hora and Niborio: which is why I saw so many dawns.

Many a time on Andros I looked toward the east and to the mythological past and saw inconstant, young and lovely Eos, third rosy-fingered child of the Titans, slip quietly from her husband's couch and rise into the sky saffron-robed and on a purple chariot, tilting her urn from which fell the morning dew, and driving the night away.

There was a particularly beautiful dawn the first time I landed at Athens airport. Part of the price one pays when travelling on the cheap is to fly by night and arrive at ungodly hours, but despite my eyes being sticky through lack of sleep it was then that I realized fully why the Ancient Greeks worshipped light. In Greece it has a marvellous quality which I have not seen equalled in any part of the world. But exhilarating though they were, those fresh cool virgin hours, and in no way minimizing the beauty of the daytime, it was the evenings and the nights that I remember best on Andros and in Hora, for it was then that my social life and further education began – in the tavernas.

Very early during my first visit to the island I learned one important fact: the taverna owner is fiercely independent. He has what I believe to be a wholly desirable philosophy, namely that neither work nor money should rule his life and, as I discovered, if he does not consider you warrant his attention or his culinary skills, meagre though they may be, you will not get them. Indeed, if at first sight a taverna owner comes to the conclusion that the two of you are just not made for each other, it is as well to quit with dignity and go to bed and lie down with an empty stomach than remain seated while he prowls around the table muttering, 'I tell you no fish, no meat

Wherever I went there was a cat

balls, no bread, no – damn-all.' When one can actually see and smell the declared unobtainables sizzling in the kitchen as the denial of their existence is being proclaimed it can be very bad for the ego.

The taverna proprietor is also a man of whims, of sudden fancies. If one arrives at his establishment when an international football match is being televised or at the precise moment that he and his family should have their meal – and this can happen at any time that he has become bored with watching others eat – one must accept the arbitrary decision gracefully, subdue the rumbling protestations of one's stomach, and wait. On such occasions one should try to seat oneself within a yard or two of the family table. A good slip fielder in form, or anyone with quick reflexes, can often get a substantial meal on the house or, to be more exact, on the shirt; the Greeks are delightfully uninhibited and enjoy their meals in a manner in which the British do not, or cannot. I think Philippedes put it in a nutshell at a dinner party when, in a voice muffled with moussaka, he said: 'You know, Yanni, for my opin – oh! So sorry, Yanni, so sorry, here take my handkerchief. For my opinion the big, big difference between English eating habituals and the Greek eating habituals is that your peoples make it seem like a duty and my peoples make it sound like a pleasure.'

There was, I felt, an echo of Sophoclean wisdom about the statement. I believe it to be true. Also on reflection I am convinced that the Hellenic antonym of 'Remember, Mr Manners, dear, never speak with your mouth full' is: 'Recollect what Socrates said, my lamb – never let a meatball halt your flow of eloquence.' Nor would a Greek Nanny fail to tell her charge that the fork is not merely an instrument for impaling victuals but a vital piece of equipment in the course of everyday mealtime conversation. Going to table in some of the less sophisticated islands is not unlike entering the lists.

All these revelations were made to me at Petros's – the taverna some fifteen yards from the shore and quite close to my pension.

Petros was a fisherman but Petros did not fish. Petros disliked fish, and he disliked fishing – in truth, Petros disliked work of any kind. He had a roly-poly wife, two roly-poly children, three roly-poly stomachs, a suspect motor-cycle and was devoted to them all. When not in bed with the first he rode uncertainly upon the last and was, I think, supremely content with both. During the Greek holiday period he employed a cook from the near-by island of Tinos to cater for the visitors from Athens and other parts, and out of season he saw to it that that role was filled, albeit unenthusiastically, by his wife or his Aged Mother. He was a good, simple, Punchinello of a man, with a big nose, no bottom teeth and he was immensely likeable.

Every evening, shortly after sunset, I would walk the gentle sand-sprayed curve of road and, bending my head under the overhanging fig-trees, scuff my way to Petros's for my one square meal of the day. Sometimes he was open by the time I arrived and sometimes he was not, in which case Aged Mother, who was at least a hundred and fifty, would mutter away to wake him; but it did not matter. It had not taken me long to realize that to Petros time was an idea in the mind of God. Secondly, the evenings were warm, there was always the scent of honeysuckle in the air and the timeless Aegean stretched in front of me. There was no cause to fret.

I would take a metal-framed and cloth-backed chair, place it in front of the open but untended door to face the sea and watch the moon rise, round and huge as an under-ripe orange. And there I would wait while the moths began their fluttered square dance round the ballroom of the outside lamp. But Petros always turned up in the end, yawning and scratching and rubbing his eyes. Then, together we would go into his kitchen and see what he had to offer – a custom which I am longing to put into practice in this country – and with luck I would eat within the hour.

My stomach was nearly always silenced by the same menu: fish if anyone had the energy to catch it or, to be more accurate, if Petros had overcome inertia to go and buy it between ouzos, meatballs if he had not, huge salads of tomatoes and cucumbers and onions, and vast helpings of bread and cheese. Once in a moment of mental aberration he did acquire some crayfish which he cooked superbly and on which I supped for three consecutive and consequently sleepless nights, but on the whole no element of surprise came from the kitchen: that ingredient was supplied by the clientèle.

Supper time at Petros's was sometimes irksome; but it was never ever boring.

CHAPTER VI

Andros Andio

I SPENT SOME wonderful evenings at Petros's, ruining my digestion but improving my knowledge of Greek and the Greeks. There was a marvellous ambience in that taverna – it was a happy place, no matter whether it was almost empty or, as on one occasion, filled to capacity with a ferry-load of overweight Womble women from Tinos. Fat, jolly souls they were, with prodigious thirsts and straining corsets. Uproariously they danced and shuddered and shrieked to the accompaniment of a minute third-rate tenor they had brought with them, complete with an accordion. He sang Neapolitan songs in a dreadful voice. Eventually he became incapable of supporting the instrument and, with the penultimate verse of 'Santa Lucia' in its death throes, sank under its weight and into oblivion beneath the table. Shortly after that they left, bearing the stricken one with them, and still singing, but not before they had shaken hands with everything that moved and asked God to bless it. I have no idea to what sorority they belonged. What was beyond doubt was their genuine warmth and friendliness; but that was always made plain to me at Petros's.

I would never sit alone for long. Sooner or later unceremoni-

ously Petros would bang a bottle on the table, point toward
the donors who would raise their glasses in salutation and I
would respond. 'Isigha!' I would shout across the room,
'Isigha!' they would bellow back 'Isigha – Ela! Come!' And
over I would go to their table and spend the rest of the evening
with them talking in a mixture of English, Greek and mime.
Somehow we got through to each other and were strangers no
longer. I met a great many people that way; including Mr
Diddley Diddley Opoulos.

I never did find out his correct name but he was a bald-
headed bespectacled man who, attached to a large bottle,
appeared at my table, cleared his throat and speaking at great
speed in a high-pitched staccato voice said: 'Good evening
and welcome and – excuse me. My name is Diddley Diddley
Opoulos and I am here for two days from Athens and I am
sitting, over-there-with-my-friend.' He pointed toward a
corner table occupied by a very large blond man, almost
entirely surrounded by bottles, whose eyes appeared to be in
vigorous competition over which direction they should look.

'He is,' said Diddley Diddley Opoulos, quite unnecessarily
and with masterly understatement, 'a little drunk but, he-
finds-you-very-desirable. Also,' he continued, unmindful of my
apprehension, 'he wishes that you join us to answer questions
about England what-he-thinks-he-love. You will come, yes?'

I took another look at his friend. He was in his early thirties,
well muscled and, on second inspection, proved much larger
than I first thought: even when sober he could, I reflected, be
capable of turning quite nasty if frustrated.

'I should be delighted,' I said.

'Enchanted,' said Diddley Diddley; and piloted me across
the room.

'Ahh!' said the besotted Anglophile in a muffled voice and
rising unsteadily, 'Ahh – kalispera!'

'Kalispera,' I said, extending my hand.

'Kaliss-pera,' he repeated, missing it by a foot and catching me in the solar plexus.

'Exactly,' said Diddley Diddley, tapping him into an upright position and assuming the dual role of plenipotentiary and interpreter, 'or as we should say, good evening.'

Spurred by the challenge, his friend rose to the occasion. 'Gudfning,' he said; and sat down heavily and astonished by what his legs had done.

'Quite,' said Diddley Diddley, clearing his throat again, 'indeed – quite; but-now-to-begin-things. This is my friend Mr Bratodoly-doodley-doodley-medes but call him Dimitrius. And-your-name-is-plis?'

'John,' I said sitting uneasily on the edge of my chair.

'Ahh!' said Dimitrius, leering happily and pouring a little wine into my glass and a great deal on to the table, 'Ah John! John! Is good, yes. John! Yes, is nice!' His left eye had a brief conference with the right one, disagreed with it, returned beaten to its own corner and he topped up his beer with retsina. 'Yes,' he said, 'is nice. Yasas John!' He drained the mixture in one, belched and fell off his seat.

'Ahem!' said Diddley Diddley, helping him back and calling the class to attention once more, 'quite. Indeed-quite. And my friend Dimitrius has not much English, not-like-me, but understands a little.

'Ahh, yes,' roared Dimitrius, his eyes revolving like oranges in a fruit machine and administering a general libation with a fresh bottle, 'yes, understand plenty, yes! Liverpool! Yes! Soho, yes! Girls! And er –' He paused, frowning with concentration and his mouth wide open. Then – 'Ahh, yes!' he said, smacking his hand triumphantly on my knee and beaming as the mental block was removed – 'Franch Laitur!'

Diddley Diddley looked blank. 'Franch Laitur?' he inquired,

'Franch Laitur? I do not know this, Franch Laitur!' He entered into rapid Greek with Dimitrius. 'Ah,' he said, when the exchange came to an end, 'now I understand. Exactly. Indeed-quite. Most precisely. Yes, my friend Dimitrius is available with the all the popular phrases. Ahem! But also,' he added, clearly wishing to raise the level of conversation, 'also my friend Dimitrius is a hunter.'

'Really,' I said, 'a hunter?'

'Yes,' said Diddley Diddley, 'a hunter. A very fine and accurate hunter.'

'Well, well, well,' I said, suitably impressed, 'what does he hunt?'

'Pigeons,' said Diddley Diddley, 'he shoots pigeons; also he makes fireplaces. Also,' he continued, 'he is, ahem! very-fond-of-girls; but here is the snugs. He is finding that Greek girls are all fart, all – excuse me, all big, here, and here and, all places, but English girls he thinks are not enlarged in these regions. And so,' said Diddley Diddley, resting his index finger and bringing the demonstration to a close, 'my friend Dimitrius wants to know how to get to Soho to meet shallow English girls – that is his burning want, indeed-quite; that is the information he wishes mostly from you.'

Dimitrius gazed at me glassily in trust and anticipation and put his arm round my neck. 'Nice John,' he said, holding me in a head lock, 'Nice John.' I hated the thought of disillusioning him.

'Well,' I said to Diddley Diddley and disengaging myself with some difficulty, 'I'm not sure but I think most of the girls in Soho are Greek, and,' I added, rubbing salt into the wound, 'very enlarged, everywhere.'

There was a terrible silence. 'Oh!' said Diddley Diddley, and relayed the dreadful news.

I do not think I have ever seen anyone look quite so sad as

'he is, ahem! very-fond-of-girls'

Dimitrius did when his hedonistic dreams of Mecca were shattered. For the remainder of the evening he slumped in his chair shaking his head at me in reproach and disbelief and being comforted by Diddley Diddley. In the next few days, I thought, the pigeons would have a thin time of it. I did not meet them again for neither was present the following night. But Tassos was.

Unlike the previous evening, the taverna was not particularly busy when Tassos loomed into my life. I was enjoying a perfectly good bottle of cheap resinated table wine called Morea and waiting for my meal to materialize when he detached himself from a group of men in the kitchen who were arguing with Petros about the merits of a large swordfish with which they had arrived, ambled across to my table and stood over me with his feet astride and his arms akimbo.

'Ya,' he rumbled and gestured disapprovingly toward the bottle, 'what for hell you drink that, eh? That no good krasi - wine. That mad Athina – chemics filth. No good! Mak stoomick go – oicks! Oicks,' he repeated, 'plenty oicks! You want for to go oick,' he inquired after the encore, 'you want for to sicks?'

I shook my head vigorously, 'No,' I said, 'oche.'

'Bravo,' said Tassos, pleased that his performance had been appreciated, 'bravo! Then you not drink her – you drink, doppio! Doppio! You understand doppio?' Again I shook my head.

'Doppio,' boomed Tassos, seating himself and harpooning one of my meatballs which had arrived during the interval, 'doppio is, mad house – mad house with graps and feet. Graps and feet,' he repeated, rising and trampling imaginary grapes in a circuit of the table and bringing the debate about the swordfish to an end, 'graps and feet! No chemics – all good! You drink all night, all day and no – er, er ponokefalo,

ponokefalo! – you understand ponokefalo?' I looked blank. He drummed with both fists upon his head. 'Yes,' he roared as I got it in one, 'bravo! – hid ark. No hid ark in bloody morning.'

He turned and delivered what I took to be a resumé of Acts 1 and 2 to the rest of the audience who gave a chorus of unqualified approval. 'And now,' he said, as the applause died down, 'I bring you doppio and we all drink – all the bodies drink Tassos's doppio. Now, I went.' And he did. All the way to his village; and unfortunately all the way back. He returned with three quart bottles.

Until that evening I had always had a sneaking sympathy for Icarius the wine maker from Attica who was murdered by hung-over shepherds whom he had made drunk, but if his concoction was remotely like Tassos's I can only say that he richly deserved his fate. Maybe it was the quality of the grapes or perhaps it had been a bad year for feet – I shall never know – but tarragon vinegar was nectar compared with Tassos's doppio. But once again I did my stuff for England until eventually, as the third bottle was broached and when no one could notice, I turned an ungrateful back on the happy company, slipped into the night and with only the moon for witness let the wine of Tassos join the sea.

The next morning I saw Tassos again. 'Yasas, Yanni!' he bellowed, 'kala? Endaxi – okkay?'

'Endaxi,' I said, 'okkay.'

'Bravo,' said Tassos, 'truth, yes – no hid ark, eh? No hid ark with doppio.'

I nodded. 'No,' I said, quite truthfully, 'no hid ark,' but I lacked the heart to tell him that I had not given his theory a chance: it would have hurt him most dreadfully.

He was a Macedonian who lived in nearby Apikia but kept his fishing boat in Niborio, a thick-set, hairy bull of a man of some forty years with dark flashing eyes and close-cropped curly hair. Strong, jet-black eyebrows and a moustache grew from a face which looked as if it had been carved from teak and his voice matched the image. Tassos never spoke in anything but a bellow, and when he laughed, which he did readily, the cliffs trembled. He radiated power and, like most Greek males I met in the islands, he was manifestly proud of his masculinity. He had huge charm and as with so many powerful men he was wonderfully gentle. And he was kind. I became indebted to him.

It was he who showed me the island from the sea. But for Tassos and his boat I would not have seen the coruscating shoals of tiny fish swimming in their millions in the electric blue-green shallows near the shores, nor sailed around black shining rocks which, towering like fossilized gods from Olympus, stood sentinel to the coast line; nor would I have known the delights of sipping sweet black coffee from small thick cups after a swim in crystal waters in little coves only accessible from the sea, where the only sounds were those of the surf and the cries of sea birds. And all these pleasures came about as a result of my first meeting with him on the night following Dimitrius's disenchantment with Soho.

They were wonderful times, those autumn days. My diary of them is very precious to me, and when I reread it the sparse, disjointed jottings of the daily happenings come alive and I relive the events as if they happened yesterday: like the Feast of the Pig. I am still uncertain as to its significance but it was a poignant occasion. It was a feast to which Petros invited me, to join his family, relatives and close friends; a feast where, for four hours, thirty or more of us sat down and ate pig and nothing but pig – the whole of the animal was presented in one delicious form or another from soup to curly tail. For four, glorious, pig-sodden hours we ate and drank and talked and laughed, sang and danced, and buffooned the night away.

We were heavy with pig, happy with pig. It was an evening I shall never forget – not because of the food and drink but for the aura it engendered – the simple warmth and friendship given to a lunatic Englishman with a poor command of Greek – ingredients which no amount of drachmae could buy.

When it was all over and the last of the walking wounded had been given assistance I walked slowly, very slowly, back to my pension, supremely content with the world; but I did not go in directly. It was a lovely night and still warm, and so I stood there, leaning against a pillar smoking a last pipe and listening to the high-pitched pip-pip-pipping of bats as they radared their ways through the dark under a sky pregnant with stars. The heavens were ablaze with them that night, sparkling like gems on jeweller's velvet and all so close, or so it seemed, that all I had to do was to stretch out my hand, pluck them from their setting one by one, put them in a bag and pay my way with them to Paradise. And, unashamed romantic that I am, as I gazed upward, lost in their beauty, I understood more perfectly the inspired words of Ptolomeus of Alexandria written centuries before.

'I know,' he wrote, 'I know well I am mortal, a feeble thing and fleeting; yet when I watch the wheelings of myriad star on star, my feet touch earth no longer. It is as I were eating, at the high God's own table, of Heaven's ambrosia.'

And so I stayed, happy and lost in the past and reading the mythologies of ancient Greece in the book of the sky. Gods and goddesses, heroes and heroines, beasts and men, all were there, their figures outlines in stars. At my back was the Plough of which Homer wrote, cutting its endless furrow around the Pole and counterbalanced by the misshapen W of Cassiopeia as she swung in her chair, doomed to circle the skies until the end of time, never rising, never setting. There was the Milky Way, that river of light from far distant stars which men in years gone by saw as the burning cindered track of Phaeton's catastrophic ride in Apollo's chariot of the Sun; the Lyre of Orpheus with which he wooed Eurydice and played to Pluto in the Underworld, there it was fixed to the sky with diamond studded nails; and to the west the semi-circle of the Northern Crown which Bacchus gave to Ariadne long ago on near-by Naxos shone as an eternal reminder of his love . . . I watched them until eventually thin cloud began to smudge the pictures and then I went to bed; but it had been a strange feeling, standing on modern Greece and looking back to the Heroic Age.

I paid two more visits to Andros after my first autumnal one – in the following spring and a more brief one in the early winter of that year: I stayed five days with Philippedes to celebrate our name day. The Greeks do not celebrate their birthdays as we do but the day of the saint after whom they are named; John the Baptist day is in January.

John is a popular name in Greece. Call out 'Yanni' in any crowded street anywhere and half the male population will acknowledge it. In Hora that day, sixty-three Yannis and their families packed the church in the early morning: but Philippedes and I were late arrivals – by design; he respects his Maker but not the Church. 'I am not,' he said, as we paused at the entrance and listened to the intoning from within, 'a very good, how to say, customer here. I do not care for the priests. They have, for my opinion, too much power, but it is good that I should be seen here today.' He is a singularly honest man and free from cant, but a great supporter of traditionalism.

Forty minutes later we breathed air and not incense. Philippedes inhaled deeply and gave a sigh of relief. 'So, Yanni,' he said as a band of Yannis streamed past us on their ways to their homes, 'bravo! That now is behind us – now for, as you might say, the real business! Now, soon you will see what a Yanni day is in Andros!'

I did. From breakfast onward every Yanni visited the house of every other Yanni. In every Yanni house there was a laden table prepared by a Yanni wife, in every house a different wine. Each Yanni home was filled with male Yanni friends who plundered the dishes and emptied decanters with a gusto which left me guessing. 'Hronia pollá!' we called to each other, 'many years', 'na zisate! – may you live!' It was hard going and by one o'clock I was not sure if I would. At four o'clock and with sixteen Yannis to my credit I retired hurt to Philippedes's flat. Unlike most of my namesakes and without their experience I had not paced myself, but by six o'clock I had got my second wind; and I am glad I did.

As I emerged from my bedroom ready for battle once more a band of happy Yannis adulterated with two Yiorgos, an Alexander, a Hercules and an Andonis, and led by Philippedes, came singing up the stairs to be greeted by Metaxia at the top. Then, into the dining-room they poured and there we sang – drank, ate and sang until midnight. And what voices they had! Tenors, baritones and basses – all blended in effortless perfect harmony to the accompaniment of two guitars to sing the songs of the Cyclades and of old Andros, songs not to be found on any commercial discs. I have never known time pass so quickly.

When they had left Metaxia lit a cigarette and exhaled wearily but happily. Two days' preparation had gone into that evening for her Yanni, but it had been worth the effort. Effacingly she had remained in the background, stage-managing the proceedings. At no time did the table lack wine; as fast as one dish was emptied so it was replenished. That had been her rôle and she had fulfilled it. That was the custom. Tomorrow she and all the other Yanni wives would put on their best dresses and visit each other's houses and she would hold court in hers. That was the custom in Andros, a tradition left over from the days when most of the island's men were away at sea for much of the year and the women kept safe company together.

Philippedes looked at her affectionately. 'Each year,' he said to me as he squeezed her hand, 'I tell her not to do too much but always she does, always she does. It is the tradition Yanni, the tradition. And you, my friend, have had the sharing. Three chars for Saint John!'

It is some time now since I last saw the island, my first love of the Cyclades. I have wanted to return but I have resisted the temptation: too many islands remain to be seen, and even allowing for the miracles which science can perform I doubt if I shall live long enough to know more than a dozen; but I shall never forget Andros and its sights and sounds and people and places. Apikia in the hills and Niborio and Hora on the coast. Apikia where in the autumn the olive groves are rich with fallen fruit; when unwashed clouds begin to hide the mountain tops and sun and the first chill comes into the wind as it blows through the cypress trees; when thunder rolls and rumbles round the hills like a petulant giant trying to find his exit and rain surprises the dry earth and a myriad sleeping scents awake and fill the air with their freshness.

All that I shall remember: just as I shall hold the memory of Niborio in the spring when lizards laze in the noonday sun and undemanding little flowers bloom in the clefts of rocks, and paths under overhanging cliffs are red with fallen poppy petals; and I can feel still the bite of winter gales when the seas are lashed to foaming fury and no one can leave the island. Nor shall I forget the narrow streets of Hora where, regardless of the season, every living being seems aware that time is a man-made thing and life is not; that life was meant for living and not mere existence and that to stop and chat inconsequentially is not a sin. But, above all, I shall remember the people of Andros.

I hated the day I left Hora for the port of Gavrion to catch the ferry to Rafina on the mainland and so back to England. Saying goodbye has never come easily to me and there were so many goodbyes to make that day, to men and women – so many unshaven cheeks to embrace, free from inhibition. I know now what emotional hedgehogs must go through – the average male in the islands shaved but once a week, on Saturdays, and as my departure took place on a Friday it did call for a degree of stoicism on my part; but I would not have had it otherwise.

Four people saw me into the bus in the square. 'Goodbye,' said Philippedes, kissing me on both cheeks, 'for my opinion this is, how to say, the tragics.' 'Ahh!' roared Tassos, doing likewise and adding a bear hug, 'doppio, eh? No hid ark eh?' 'Andio,' said Leonardo and Petros as they loofahed my face simultaneously, 'kalo taksithe ke o Theos masisas – bon voyage and God be with you'; and we all wept over each other.

By the wall of the bus station a large, rawboned, pink and newly arrived Glaswegian eyed the scene with undisguised disgust. 'Dear God, Nully,' he said to his wife, 'ded youse see tha'? Dear, dear, dear – they're everywhere these days!'

I climbed into the bus feeling like a small boy going away to school for the first time, squeezed into a seat between an incensed-scented priest and a fat lady smelling strongly of assorted cheeses, and waved to the quartet through the back window; and I kept on waving until I could see them no longer.

The priest turned to me and smiled. 'Friends,' he said in stilted English, 'good friends with love – that is when life is real good.'

I nodded. And as the bus bumped and rattled its way snaking first uphill and then down en route for Gavrion, and I looked out at the silver grey of the underside of the olive leaves as they twisted toward the sun, I knew I was leaving behind not acquaintances – but friends; and that thought was still with me when I boarded the ferry and remained with me as we chugged farther and farther away. And as I watched the wake grow longer and the island smaller I knew that I would have to return – one day; but when I did so it would not be as a stranger.

A month after my return and with the chill of an approaching English winter beginning to eat into my bones I sat with a much-travelled friend of mine looking at a map of the Aegean spread on the floor in front of us. There against the blue and between the mainlands of Greece and Turkey with Crete at the bottom of the page lay the scattered chips of the Cyclades and the Dodecanese. One by one my friend dismissed the better known islands of both groups. 'They're beautiful,' he said, 'of course they are – all Greece is beautiful; but they're not for you; but there's a place which hasn't been discovered – yet.' And he pointed to the name, Kardamena: it was on the island of Kos.

'Kardameena?' I said, mis-pronouncing the word.

'No,' said my friend, 'Kardamena.'

'Sounds vaguely Turkish,' I said.

'Well it isn't,' he said, although as the crow flies Kos isn't all that far from Turkey and there are traces of past Turkish influence on the island.

'Is it like Andros,' I asked, 'like Hora and Niborio?'

He shook his head. 'Not in the least,' he said. 'By comparison with Kardamena, Hora's sophisticated. There's money in Hora – there isn't in Kardamena. You won't find any banks there – and you certainly won't find a Philippedes.'

'No,' he went on, 'it's a fishing village of simple people. Good, simple, kind people who laugh a lot and who, you'll find, will welcome you collectively.' He paused. 'And I'll tell you what else you'll find there – apart from good retsina: characters. You'll have to go a long way before you meet as many characters as you will in Kardamena.'

He started to fold the map up. 'At least,' he said, 'that's what I found; but go and see for yourself. April's a good month.'

Spring seemed a long time coming . . .

PART TWO

CHAPTER I

Dogged by Gogs

'K os,' so a guide book advised me, 'is the home of the
famous Kos lettuce and it is also the birthplace of Hippo-
crates who founded a medical school there.' Patently the
publication envisaged a catholic readership and was intent upon
interesting both the agricultural student and the amateur
classicist, to say nothing of members of the National Health
Service. However, it was neither salad nor science which drew
me to Kos but the promise that part of it at least still remained
comparatively unknown to the tourist: which is why, on the
morning of April 28th, 1977, I flew from Gatwick en route for
the fishing village of Kardamena on the southern coast of the
island.

In those days and at that time of the year the only way to get
to Kos was by 'plane to Rhodes and thence by a five-hour
ferry journey – now one can fly direct; but I remember that
flight to Rhodes very clearly, not only because of the number
of advanced geriatrics aboard which prompted me to wonder
how many would actually walk off the aircraft to enjoy their
holiday, but also because of a young woman, whose baggage
tags announced that she was going to Lindos. Aged about

thirty, she was wearing a huge, white, cowboy-type hat worthy of the worst extravagances of Ascot, white ear-rings and large dark glasses, and a neck scarf clearly labelled 'Harrods – seventeen pounds, thirty-five'. She was three rows ahead of me on the left of the aircraft and sat sideways in the aisle seat with one arm draped languidly along the back of it and her legs stretched across the gangway. Throughout the journey she crossed and uncrossed them, swinging them gently up and down and slowly rotating a high-heeled shoe on her toes. I am sure she brightened the lives of a mesmerised few, but she earned the undying hatred of the cabin crew and the less continent of the elderly who found their way to the rear of the aircraft obstructed.

Somewhere over Switzerland she lost the shoe. Gallantly it was retrieved by an octogenerian who handed it to her with a little bow. 'Ta-er, thenks,' she said, 'thenks ever so.'

Neither the hasty correction nor the half-polished phrase went unnoticed. Across the aisle and level with me a sixty-year-old lady with a severe face and a hairnet sniffed and ground her peppermint to dust. 'Snff!' she said, 'Ernie's come up for someone hasn't he just?' 'Pools more like it,' said her blue-rinsed companion, 'no better than she ought to be if you ask me. Huh! Harrods indeed! Common as muck! And look at them nails!'

Contrary to what most people say I never find air travel boring: tedious yes, but never boring.

We touched down at Rhodes airport on time, gaggled our way across the tarmac to passport control, then to reception and into the arms of divers couriers from travel agencies. Eleven of us were met by a charming tubby one-eyed Greek named George. I had lunched with him in London some months earlier and we greeted each other warmly. Completely un-flappable, George was an Anglophile with near perfect English and a dry sense of humour. Harrods, however, was not of our number; other arms awaited her.

'Cukla mu!' roared an enormous and immensely virile Greek as he bore down upon her with open arms and bristling moustachios, 'Cukla mu, how good, how bloody good to see you – the boat is ready and so am Hi!'

'Eau Nikko, daurling!' squealed Harrods in unashamed anticipation, allowing herself to be squeezed off her feet and flailing her legs as she did so, 'Eau Nikko you are the end, you are rahly! Eau Nikko! Nikko!! – mind me 'at!'

'See what I mean?' said blue rinse to the peppermint addict, 'no better than she ought to be! Didn't I say that Gladys – didn't I say that?'

'You did,' said Gladys, using her incisors like an outraged rabbit and reducing another lozenge to powder, 'you did. Disgusting, that's what it is, disgusting!'

'Quite,' said a large, redfaced and hirsute lady with pointed ears who, with an equally large and bucolic husband had sat in front of me in the 'plane. 'Quite! Don't you think so Gog? GOG!'

Her husband started violently as she struck him in the ribs. He had watched the legshow with unwavering concentration and an increasing pulse rate from take-off to landing and was still under its spell. 'Oh yes,' he said in a low voice, 'yes. Yes I do, yes,' and continued to breathe heavily.

'I think,' said George, preventing further character assassination and speculation, 'that it's time to go. Please ladies and gentlemen go to the orange coach with white lettering. I repeat: the orange coach with white lettering. Your bags are already on board and I will be with you in one minute.' He caught me by the arm. 'Yanni,' he said, 'there is a small problem but don't worry, I must –' He broke off abruptly. 'Oh God,' he said, 'look;' and raised his voice to the disappearing crocodile: 'No! The *orange* coach with the *white* lettering not the white with the – yes sir, that's right, the *orange* coach.' He looked after them and wiped his eye. 'You know,' he said, 'I have a feeling that some of them will die on the hoof. Come on – I will explain in a minute.'

I seated myself halfway down the coach and watched George take his position next to the driver and go into action with a hand microphone.

'Ladies and gentlemen,' he began, 'welcome officially to the beautiful island of Rhodos. Now for those of you who are spending your holiday here I have very good news: nothing has gone wrong. However,' he continued, 'for those of you who are not staying here the news is not so good – there is no ferry tomorrow morning for the other islands.'

In front of me Gog and Magog stiffened in their seats.

'What!' said Gog belligerently, 'no ferry?'

'No ferry,' said George.

'Why?' asked Gog, looking as if he was about to strike ten.

'I don't know,' said George, 'but I think it has been impoonded.'

'Impoonded?' shrilled Magog.

'Yes,' said George, 'impoonded. Somewhere along the line I think a cheque has boonced.'

It was then that I knew that I was back. Nowhere in the world are ferries impoonded with such regularity as they are in Greece, mainly, I believe, because there is no other country where rival shipping firms employ such Machiavellian methods to prevent each other from earning a dishonest living; but there we are – it is all part of the charm of the place and somehow it would seem quite wrong if that promise of uncertainty was removed. However, my philosophy was not shared.

'Ridiculous!' said Gog, half rising in his seat and returning to it suddenly as we took a bend.

'Not good enough!' said Magog doing likewise.

'We shall complain,' said Gog rising again like a yoyo, 'you can depend on that my good man, we shall complain!'

His good man looked at him. 'I'm sorry,' he said, 'it is not my fault and not my company's – it is life.'

Near to me an elderly passenger wearing a panama hat adjusted his hearing appliance, 'What's the matter with those two?' he bellowed to his companion with a similar device. 'Not sure,' quavered his friend, 'but I think they want to get orf.'

Thirty minutes later and with Gog and Magog still un-mollified by the assurance that all their expenses for an extra night in Rhodes would be met in full plus the promise of an excursion the following day, we decamped at our hotel and George departed with the deaf-aided to another resting place. I booked in, took a shower and then used the remainder of the afternoon and early evening to explore Rhodes: it is a beautiful city and on one occasion I actually heard Greek spoken.

At nine o'clock, and by arrangement, I met George in his office. He was still working.

'Sit down,' he said, 'ouzo?' I nodded. He poured two, added water and we clinked glasses and drank. George set his glass down heavily on his desk. 'Sometimes,' he said, 'I wonder why I do this job.'

'Ah! – too much paper work?' I asked.

'No,' he said, 'not that, but today has been a day! I've been shouted at by Germans, cursed by the French, attacked by Egyptians and threatened by Danes. All that I can take – but to be abused by the English deaf because I could not renew their bloody batteries on the spot is too much! But anyway,' he continued, finishing his drink, 'let us go now and eat at a taverna not dedicated to soaking the tourist; believe it or not there are such places.'

There are: and we ate in one in a village not four miles from the town. The food was superb, some of the best I have eaten in Greece. The price was reasonable and there was not a tourist in sight. We discussed the tourist industry at large and the benefits and problems it presented to both our countries.

'Beautiful though it is,' I said, 'Rhodes is not my cup of tea.'

'No,' said George, 'but you should come here in the winter – then the hot dogs and hamburgers go underground, and then with more time on my hands I could show you villages and communities which are truly Greek in spirit. Which reminds me,' he said, 'I must organize something for the unlovely English couple in your hotel – I've told them I shall see them at ten tomorrow morning. But don't worry,' he said reassuringly, sensing my anxiety, 'we shall not be together with them. No, I think I shall allow a colleague of mine to have the pleasure of their company for the day – *I* will be *your* servant.' He paused. 'Incidentally,' he said, 'they too are going to Kardamena.'

'Oh, no!' I said.

'Oh, yes!' said George, 'who's a lucky boy then?' He yawned. 'Bed I think, Yanni, ne? Let's go.'

We parted under the walls of the city's castle and I walked past the massed moorings of private motor yachts at anchorage, past the still crowded cafés and gift-shops on the front and back to my hotel. Standing in the foyer were Gog and Magog. They were like twin pillars of doom.

'This place,' said Gog sepulchrally when he saw me, 'is full of Swedes. Swedes,' he repeated sibilantly, 'I can't stand Swedes. Never could.'

'No,' I said, 'nor can I – not even with butter.'

He eyed me balefully. 'That is not in the least funny,' he said.

'No!' said Magog, 'not in the least.'

The following morning, just after ten o'clock, I looked out through the windows of the hotel's entrance hall, watching for George's arrival. Presently two cars drew up. George got out of one and the driver of the second, a tall pleasant-looking blond man, joined him on the pavement. For a minute they engaged in earnest conversation accompanied by much arm waving and during which the blond man looked progressively less and less pleasant. The tête-à-tête ended with George patting his companion on the shoulder in what appeared to me to be a gesture of sympathy and together they came through the swing doors.

'Ah,' said George, when he saw Gog and Magog who were standing near by, 'good morning to you! And good morning to you too, Yanni. I hope you have all slept well?'

'No,' said Gog, ponderously, 'I did not! I was bitten by mosquitoes. All night; and in several places.'

'Mosquitoes?' said George.

'Mosquitoes,' said Gog. 'And my wife was bitten also; all over!'

'*All* over?' said George incredulously.

'All *over*,' repeated Gog.

'But,' said George, 'I don't understand – were you perhaps er, on top of the bed – that is, without a cover?'

Magog looked at him coldly. 'I have never slept uncovered in my life,' she said.

'Never!' confirmed her husband. 'And I must tell you, we shall complain!'

'Strongly,' said Magog. 'And what is more, if they go septic, we shall sue.'

'Of course,' said George diplomatically, 'of course, I quite understand. But now,' he said, turning to his companion, 'may I introduce my colleague who will be looking after you today. I was,' he continued, avoiding my eye, 'telling him about you just before we came in. His surname is unpronounceable but his first name is Rolfe.'

'Rolfe?' said Gog, turning the name in his mouth like a hot plum, 'Rolfe! That is not a Greek name surely?'

'No,' said Rolfe, 'I am Swedish.'

Gog looked at him malevolently. 'Oh,' he said, 'are you!'

'Yes,' said Rolfe, drawing heavily on his hidden reserves of Scandinavian charm, 'and I am at your service willingly for the day. We shall, I know, have a good time together. I thought I would like to take you to –'

'We want,' interrupted Gog, 'to go to the Valley of Butterflies!'

'Ah,' said Rolfe, 'the Butterfly Valley – yes, it is very beautiful but I thought it would be better if we go instead to Kamiros because –'

'Surely,' said Gog, raising his voice, 'after all we have gone through we can go where *we* want to go and not where *you* want?'

'Of course,' said Rolfe, 'but –'

'Then,' thundered Gog, 'take us to the Butterfly Place!'

We watched them drive off.

'We all,' said George, 'have our little cross to bear but in Rolfe's case I think the splinters will stick in his hands for some time. But now, Yanni, where would you like to go? The day is yours.'

A girl walked past us, moving beautifully. She had good legs and knew it. 'What,' I said, thinking back to the Harrods display in the aircraft and her advertised journey's end, 'what about Lindos?'

The journey to Lindos was impressive. With the sea on our

'We shall complain,' said Gog. *'Strongly,'* said Magog

left we motored past green and purple mountains and through
peasant villages, then, after travelling for forty minutes, the
road climbed a hill, turned right, and bored through a rock-
face. Suddenly below us we saw Lindos – the dazzling white
houses of the village nestling in a hollow between the mainland and under its sandstone acropolis, and with a crescent of
translucent sea before it.

We stopped the car and got out. It had rained a little and the
air was fragrant and I took it deep into my lungs.

'Beautiful, isn't it?' said George.

'Breathtaking,' I said.

'Yes,' said George, 'Kensington Gore on the Aegean. But
my friend,' he said, wagging an admonishing finger, 'let us not
be cynical – the hedonists have been the salvation of Lindos.'

He plucked a grass stalk from the roadside and pointed
with it. 'Do you see those houses down there? Mediaeval,
many of them. Fifteen years ago there was dung on their floors;
now they're let to tourists – nearly all the villas are. Yes,' he
said, 'they do say that in the high season the rattle of cocktail
glasses can be heard in Rhodes when the wind's in the right
direction. And,' he continued, 'fifteen years or so ago the locals
scratched a living from the soil; now they grow fat on tourism.
Their houses are clean, so are their streets; and so are their
finger-nails. Oh yes, my friend, under those white roofs is the
gleam of gold!'

'And have they,' I asked, 'retained their old community
spirit?'

'Ah,' said George, chewing his stalk reflectively, 'I don't
know about that; but they have their Coca-Cola.'

We drove further along the road, parked, and then began
the staggered descent into the village and down the steps of
its narrow streets.

It was, as George had suggested, terribly Homes-and-

Gardens. To me, the village seemed unreal – it was a stage set in which I found it difficult to believe that real life went on; also I found the glare from the dazzling white walls of the houses painful and I was glad when we reached the beach. We sat for a while in silence and watched a plump American lady in her mid-fifties having her back oiled by a young Greek. She lay there like an overweight Cheshire cat, eyes closed and smiling into the sand. 'Paulo, dear' she purred, '*this* is divine. Just a little lower down, dear, just a *little* lower – oh! yes! – that's it, honey, mmm.' The pink fat quivered in ecstasy.

'As you see,' said George, 'there is no unemployment in Lindos.'

A flotilla of pedaloes passed in front of us and in the distance, beyond a beach planted with tufted straw shades on poles, a pleasure steamer from Rhodes disgorged its human cargo. Nearer, a bikini-clad girl appeared at the door of a small beach villa. 'Edwina,' she called, 'don't forget will you, darling – peeps for din after drinkies. Shall need a hand in the kitch!'

Four yards away a spread-eagled Edwina raised her face from her pillow. 'Balls!' she said. 'Ask Charlotte.'

George looked at me with his one good eye. 'We get,' he said, 'a very good class of person in Lindos.'

He stood up, dusted the sand from his trousers and looked in the direction of the pleasure steamer, watching the last stragglers making their way to a beach taverna. 'That's stop number one,' he said, 'the culture will come later;' and he pointed upward to the acropolis of Athena. 'That's why they come and that's where they'll go, by donkey. The Germans will remember the culture, the British will remember the donkeys and the pretty girls, Yanni,' and he paused, 'will remember the donkey boys.' I raised my eye-brows. 'Precisely,' said George.

Before we left in the cool of a late afternoon and after we had

climbed to the acropolis and looked down at yet another bay
in which St Paul was said to be shipwrecked – and there cannot
be many among the islands in which he is not supposed to have
staggered ashore, I stood by the car and had a last look at
Lindos. It was very beautiful and I was glad I had been allowed
to see it.

I swept the panorama with my binoculars, picking out the
detail of the path we had climbed, and then focused on the
little beach where we had sat. The fat, pink lady had gone, so
had her anointer, and so had Edwina; but to my intense joy,
Harrods came into view. She was still wearing her hat but she
had changed her ear-rings; and her partner. She was, as they
say, getting to know him. For her at least, I thought, Lindos
was a demi-paradise.

It had been an enjoyable day for both of us but I was tired
when George dropped me at the hotel with the promise to
meet me later. I waved to him as he drove off to his office
and went over to the reception desk to get my key. As I
turned from the counter the sun set abruptly on my day.
Sitting side by side on a bench seat and staring unseeingly into
space were Gog and Magog. They were having their evening
hate. My heart sank but it was too late to take evasive action.

'Ah,' I said, as I walked over to them, 'I hope you had a
good day?' It was a stupid question.

'We did not,' said Gog, 'we had a terrible day.'

'Quite dreadful,' said Magog.

'We had a puncture,' said Gog.

'And the spare was flat,' said his wife.

'We shall complain of course,' said Gog.

'Of course,' I said.

'Strongly,' said Magog.

'But you got there?' I asked.

'Eventually,' said Gog, 'eventually.'

'And the butterflies,' I asked, 'how were the butterflies?'

Gog looked at me through his rimless glasses, his face turning even redder. 'There were no butterflies,' he rumbled.

'Not *one*,' said Magog.

'Not a single one,' said Gog, distilling the words drop by drop, 'and do you know what that fellow said when I complained?' he continued. 'He had the impertinence to tell us we should come back in the summer because now they were only . . .' he choked on the word, 'caterpillars.'

I managed to avoid them at breakfast and providentially I did not see them at all until half past three in the afternoon when once again we assembled in the foyer and waited for George to take us to the ferry. When he arrived he made a charming little speech in which he expressed his regret for our delay but hoped that we had enjoyed our enforced stay.

'I found it wholly delightful,' said the fourth member of the party, an elderly doctor en route for Samos who had stayed with friends, 'yes, wholly delightful – indeed last night I met some awfully nice gels and we danced until – oh dear me – one o'clock I think it was, yes most pleasant – Greek style of course. Er, do you do Greek dancing?' he inquired of Gog.

Gog stared at him. 'I have bad feet,' he said.

'Oh dear me,' said the doctor, who was a bright little man with a high-pitched, crackly voice. 'Well! Well! Well! What a pity – you ought to have 'em seen to! But I wouldn't let a Greek doctor look at 'em – might lose 'em all together what?' He cackled happily at his sally.

Gog breathed heavily. 'We have already,' he said, addressing an audience of thousands, 'had sufficient deprivations,' and looked meaningly at George.

'Well,' said George, grateful for the light relief despite the slur on his country's practitioners, 'now all that is behind you – now there will be no more snags. The ferry is definitely going and will leave at about four-thirty, or five, but it doesn't matter, and that will – er should,' he corrected hastily, 'get you to Kos at about ten o'clock tonight; I hope.'

He cleared his throat. 'However, there is one very small thing I must tell you. Because of the impoonding of the other ferry and also because of the coming of May Day tomorrow – May Day is a big public holiday here – this one ferry may be just a little, just a little er, crooded. But now I wish you bon voyage or, as we say in Greece – Kalo taxithe!'

Apart from learning to speak English fluently and colloquially George has also absorbed many of our traits. Among them is the gift of understatement. We did not board the ferry – we were carried to it on the crest of a joyous babbling human tidal wave bearing camping equipment, national flags, national cheeses, piano accordions, guitars and bouzoukois. Several yards ahead of me the little doctor suddenly vanished in the sea of bodies to re-appear just as suddenly and transformed into a seven-footer.

'Ah what fun it all is,' he chirped, with his feet off the ground and beaming down at the death masks of the Gogs to his right, 'very Greek, what! Oh very Greek! Very –' and disappeared again as we all surged nearer to the gangway. When I next saw him he was sitting cross-legged on the deck with a rollicking crowd of thirty students and singing his heart out with them; I was sad he was not coming to Kos. Of Gog and Magog I saw nothing until six agonizing hours later, having sailed an hour behind schedule, the same tidal wave deposited us on the quayside at Kos. It was eleven o'clock, humid and raining gently.

An attractive girl, wearing a T-shirt emblazoned with the name of the travel agent with whom we had booked, greeted us by name and steered us toward a waiting taxi. It was small and very old; and so was its driver.

'And this,' said the girl brightly, affecting an introduction to the ancient, 'is Dimitri.'

Dimitri smiled warmly and toothlessly at us through the drizzle. 'Yasas!' he said.

'What?' said Gog.

'And Dimitri,' continued the girl even more brightly, as our cases were crammed into the boot and its lid was tied with string to the rear bumper, 'Dimitri is Stelio's brother – he's a dear.'

'Is he?' said Gog heavily.

'Yes,' said the girl chattily, as the string parted with a twang and the boot lid shot up, 'an absolute dear – you'll be comfortable with him.'

'I hope so,' said Gog ominously, watching Dimitri attempting miracles with the frayed string, 'I sincerely hope so. And are you,' he said, acknowledging my presence for the first time, 'staying there?'

'No,' I said, 'I'm booked in at a pension.' The relief was mutual.

There was another twang as the string broke for the second time.

'I hope,' said Gog, taking another jaundiced look at Dimitri, 'that it will not be long before we go.'

'Oh no,' said the girl, now brittle with brightness, 'any old moment now – eh Dimitri? Endaxi? Ne?'

Dimitri nodded vigorously. 'Umm,' he said, his gums clamped upon the string, 'Umm!'

'Jolly good,' said the girl. 'Good old Dimitri – he's a brick!' She brought a refreshing breeze of Roedean and the Sussex downs to the humidity of Kos.

'He may be,' said Gog, as steam began to rise from his anorak, 'but I am getting damp.'

Triumphantly Dimitri straightened up. 'Endaxi!' he said.

'Super!' said the girl; and we squeezed in and began the journey.

Next to me in the back seat, and wedged together in an unhappy mass, the Gogs radiated an aura of dampness and hostility. For a long while no one spoke: Gog peered gloomily into the darkness through the steamed up windows and cleared a circle with his hand.

'The countryside,' he tolled, 'appears very flat. I understood from the brochure that it was hilly. I hope,' he said, preparing a mental draft to the Association of British Travel Agents, 'that we have not been misled.'

'Oh, no,' said the girl hurriedly, assessing the wind direction accurately, 'not a bit – it's beautifully hilly in parts – marvellous climbing country; and walking too of course,' she added hastily.

'I neither walk nor climb,' said Gog; and paused. 'My feet, you know.'

'Oh!' said the girl. And gave up.

Forty minutes later we pulled up in the square of Kardamena and in the front of Hotel Stelio. A figure came quickly from the porch and jerked at the taxi door. 'Welcome!' cried Stelio, as the handle came off and the boot lid flew up, 'welcome!' he repeated, as a strong wind blew a mixture of rain and dust into our eyes: 'Welcome to Kardamena!'

CHAPTER II

Yasas! Kardamena!

O NE DOES NOT get the best impression of any place when
one is introduced to it on the stroke of midnight in the
teeth of a gale and with an empty stomach. I did not get out
of the taxi; I fell from it backwards and sideways as the support
of the door was removed.

Still clasping the door handle Stelio shook me warmly by
the hand, quickly transferred his attention to his guests who
had made a slower and more conventional exit from the other
side, and together they were blown into the shelter of his hotel.
Dimitri staggered after them with their cases, the nice girl
guided me through the rain to my pension three hundred
yards down the road, introduced me to Kosta my pensionaire
and departed.

Within minutes of my arrival I was fed with bean soup,
salami and retsina and went to bed feeling much better and
with the sound of the sea in my ears. Perhaps it was the salami
but I dreamed that the Gogs, stark naked and hand in hand
with the little doctor, were dancing around my bed.

Later that morning I woke up to find bright sunlight
filtering through the shuttered windows. I looked at my watch,
found it was nine o'clock, put on my dressing gown and took

my first look at Kardamena from the balcony of my room which overlooked the main street.

In front of me a range of flat-topped hills formed a backcloth to the turmeric coloured dome of the village church. I came to know that well in later days, and I remember it not only for the beauty of its services but because it was the only church in which I have ever seen change taken from the offertory plate. It lay well back from the shops and houses on the other side of the half-mile or so of concrete road which separated by no more than fifteen feet the flat-roofed, shuttered buildings which flanked it. Here and there a sloping roof of terracotta tiles broke the overall colour scheme of pinks and greens and whites, but there were few of them.

To my right the sliced hills gave way to blue mountains and the road ran neatly enough to the village square and to Stelio's hotel; in the other direction, as far as I could determine, it petered out into an area of oatmeal dust with a few scattered buildings and then married with a dirt track which skirted to the right.

Kardamena had been awake for some time. Below me on the opposite side of the street, and under a sign in English saying 'BICIKLES for Rent', a small man festooned with tyres and surrounded by buckets of water, pumps and an advisory committee of three was bending over one of four antiquated machines which, resting on their saddles and upright handlebars, pointed their wheels sadly to the sky. They looked very ill. As I watched he aimed a savage blow at the machine with a large adjustable spanner. It shuddered under the impact and parted with its pedals. 'Bravo!' said the advisory committee; and burst into spontaneous applause. To their right, four old men on plastic chairs momentarily lost concentration on their card game, peered rheumily in the direction of the bicycle hospital and then resumed their play.

A truck, laden with fruit and vegetables, its archaic loud-speaker stridently advertising its wares from its roof, drove slowly down the street from the direction of the square. 'Portokalia! Agouri! Lemoni! Patates! – Oranges! Cucumbers! Lemons! Potatoes! – it proclaimed tinnily and indigestibly as it Pied-Pipered its way through the village, 'Portokalia! Agouri! Lemoni!' – and came to a halt in front of Kosta's shop beneath. 'Kardamena,' I thought, as I watched the comings and goings and weighing and buying and picking and choosing, 'is all go'; and moved to the bathroom.

I turned the hot-water tap. It emitted a long, rude hiss, and lapsed into silence. I tried its fellow: that too gave a death rattle. I swore under my breath and plugged in my electric shaver. It remained dormant. I tried the light switch. Nothing happened. I used a very vulgar word indeed and went down the spiral stairs and into the street to find Kosta and met him coming away from the scrum at the vegetable cart.

'Ah,' he said waving a cucumber in greeting, 'kalimera! Kalimera! Ti kanete? Kala? 'Ave a houringe!'

'Yes, I'm very well but,' I said, clasping the gift, 'there is no water and no –'

'Ah!' said Kosta, whose English was learned during the Italian occupation of the island and further mutilated by a five-year stay in West Africa and one in Australia, 'Ah! eet ees the storma! Alwhy the storma and the whinda stoppa-the-water-and-the-juce. Alwhy! Alla, ena lepto,' he said, lapsing into Greek and then into Australian – 'Wite!' He disappeared briefly into his house and returned with a jug and a bucket. 'Rine!' he said, 'Rine from the God and the roofa! Endaxi?' I peered into the pail. Its contents were the colour of tea; but it was water.

'Endaxi,' I said, 'epharisto poli.'

'Kala,' said Kosta, 'good!' He pointed to the jug. 'So this is for the fice and this,' he indicated the pail, 'is for use of toilet.'

'But,' I said, 'surely the –'

'Ah, no! no! no!' he said, reading my unfinished sentence. 'Oche! Thenkatalavis – you naut oonderstand! Naut for sitting on or,' he paused delicately, 'you nau, but for maike with the pourings – after-the-sittings.'

From somewhere in my survival kit I unearthed an old safety razor: the colour of its blade matched that of the water but I put it to use. The bleeding stopped surprisingly quickly. A quarter of an hour later and smelling strongly of T.C.P. I went out. Across the road the bicycle doctor had abandoned his former patient and was giving the kiss of life to an inner tube. 'Yasas,' he said, and continued in Greek, 'what's your name? Ah Yanni! I'm a Yanni too.' He pointed to a convalescent leaning against the wall: 'You want a bicycle?'

'Not now,' I said, 'I'm going to have some breakfast.'

'Ah well,' he said, 'later perhaps – Yasas.' And returned to his life's work.

I left him to it and twenty yards on breakfasted off thick yoghurt and honey in a little pastry shop next to a barber. A plump, full-bosomed, motherly woman served me – a Toy-Town Apple Woman of a lady with rosy cheeks, a beaming smile and a husky chuckle and arms like legs of mutton. Her name was Sylvi and she and I and her husband, Yanni, who kept the barber's shop next door were to become firm friends. Every morning she would open her door, sweep the street outside her shop, make her yoghurt, and then plunge her great red dermatised hands into pastry mixture and conjure up sweet magic. And every day Yanni the barber, who sang tenor in the church on Sundays and who was the only man in Kardamena to shave on weekdays, whose face was pink and Tussaud's-waxy and free from worry lines, would pop in from next door, sit and sip quickly a cup of coffee, then – up again and out. He reminded me of a puppy, happy and quick and eager to please.

Sylvi refused payment that morning. 'Tomorrow,' she said. 'Today we welcome you to Kardamena – Yasas!'

I meandered further down the street, looking at the houses and watching people and generally getting the feel of the place. There seemed to be few foreign visitors, apart from the swallows. They were there in their hundreds and hardly a building was without a nest under construction, and I spent some time watching them swooping and diving between the overhead wires as they brought home the mud and kneaded it into place under the eaves: it was fun watching their houses grow and dry in the sun. Eventually I retraced my steps, past Yanni the Bicycle, whose out-patient department had grown alarmingly in the hour, bought some cheese and olives and an orange from Kosta for my lunch, refused a cup of coffee, and then set off toward the square and Stelio's. Four little girls in blue and white and wearing May Day garlands 'Yasas-ed' me as they skipped by, chattering like magpies; and so did everyone else I passed.

Stelio's hotel was very near the beach and close to a jetty along which small fishing boats bobbed up and down at anchorage, and I walked a little way along it before paying him a visit. Inshore, to my right, the cane-covered verandahs of the tavernas stretched along the front, looking out to the neighbouring volcanic islands of Yelli and Niceros; facing me, and hazy in the far distance, was Turkey; and to my left and at the end of a bay, the blue humps of the Dromas mountains reached down to the sea. Near by a middle-aged fisherman stood watching me and playing with his worry beads. 'Ine poli orea, ne?' he said, swinging the kombouloi in his hand, 'it is very beautiful, yes?'

'Very,' I said.

'Yes,' he said, 'but there is always that one shadow.' And he pointed seaward. 'Turkey,' he said; and spat. He gazed at the landmass in hostile silence for a moment, feeding and clicking the beads along the string and then looked curiously at me. 'You are, English – ne?'

I nodded.

'I thought so,' he said, 'you do not talk loudly enough to be a German. Also there is the pipe; but I find it strange that you can speak even a little Greek – you are the first Englishman I have met who tries. Bravo!'

'It is not easy,' I said.

He roared with laughter and tossed the kombouloi into the air and caught it. 'My friend,' he said, 'even the Greeks find it difficult!

'You stay with Stelio,' he asked, as we turned back.

I shook my head. 'Oche,' I said, 'but I was going to see him – I met him last night.'

'Ah, yes.' he said, 'you arrived very late in the storm with an English couple. I heard from Dimitri that they were, how to say, ready for the cemetery. But the Stelio, you will not find him, he is in Kos. He drives the bus you understand; each day he drives the bus. Ah, yes! He is a good man and works hard. Too hard. He has much trouble with his stomach because of work; but his brother is there.'

'Dimitri?' I asked.

'Oche,' he said, as he left me at the door of Stelio's entrance hall-cum-dining-room-cum-kitchen – 'Leon;' and chuckled. 'Leon! – little Leon!'

Leon was the first person I greeted when I went in. He was sitting cross-legged on a stool by the food counter noisily sipping a cup of coffee and staring hard at the terrazzo-tiled floor as he did so. He was a wizened little man with a wrinkled satyr's face and looked like an unwanted garden gnome who had lost his fishing rod; but, as I discovered, Leon always looked like that. Unlike his brother who was uncrowned king of Kardamena and a man of substance with quite a few possessions, including a rampant duodenal ulcer, Leon had no ambition. He was, I think, disillusioned with life and went through it permanently bent at a hundred degrees. Sitting opposite him in a corner, and holding a shooting stick with a rubber ferrule, was Gog.

'Ah,' I said and trying hard not to think of my dream, 'Good morning!' He looked at me as if I had uttered an obscenity.

'There was,' he intoned, 'no water this morning; nor was there electricity. And, moreover,' he continued, raising his voice above the ebb and flow of Leon's elevenses, 'that fellow over there does not understand a word I say. It is not good enough! I repeat – not nearly good enough; and I shall complain.'

'I know,' I said, 'it was a bit of a bore wasn't it? Especially shaving.'

He eyed me more closely. 'You appear to have cut yourself,' he said. 'Quite badly;' and brightened visibly. 'Yes,' he repeated, 'quite badly! Fortunately I always carry a battery operated razor. There is nothing,' he said, sounding like a commercial for the Boy Scout movement, 'like being prepared.'

'Nothing,' I said, glad that I had brought some sunshine into his life, 'I quite agree.'

'But unfortunately,' he went on as his moment of pleasure passed, 'I could not Soak My Feet.'

He paused, 'I Soak My Feet each morning,' he said.

'Good idea,' I said, 'everyone should.'

'Without fail.'

'Very wise.'

'In Fynnon Salts.'

'Really?'

'Or I use Calusolve.'

'Ah, yes, Calusolve.'

'It dissolves my callouses.'

'It would.'

'I set great store by Calusolve.'

'Of course.'

'And Fynnon Salts.'

'Quite.'

'I never travel without either. And if I cannot Soak My Feet,' he concluded gloomily, 'I cannot walk. However, my wife has gone to make inquiries about bicycles. There is, I believe, a fellow in the village who hires them?'

'Yes,' I said, 'his name is Yanni.'

'Really?' he said, clearly disapproving that I was on christian name terms with a local, 'really;' and levered himself up with his shooting stick. 'I should do something about that face of yours,' he said. 'It may go bad.' For a moment he looked almost happy.

As I turned right outside Stelio's and passed the end of the main street on my way inland toward the hills I saw the substantial figure of Magog approaching the hotel. She was perspiring freely; and wheeling two bicycles.

It did not take me long to leave the village behind – five minutes, no more – and then with the sun on my back I left the concrete road to Kos, branched off, and took a stony, dusty track across a plateau. It was lined with fig trees from which tethered goats tore the lower leaves with their sandpaper tongues, and bordered by fields either green with crops or busy with oxen pulling wooden ploughs. From small, dilapidated, grey stone buildings, chained and unkempt mongrels strained at their leashes and barked and snarled at me as I passed their preserves; but those were the only unfriendly sounds I heard.

In the fields, men and women, the latter in voluminous black skirts, their heads and lower faces shrouded in scarves, straightened up from their labours and waved. 'Poo parte?' they shouted, their feet astride and their arms akimbo, 'Where are you going?'

'Nowhere,' I shouted back, 'just walking! Para pano – up!'

'Good,' they said, 'it is beautiful in the hills – Yasas! Yasas!'

On I went. A flock of sparrows hurtled past me hedge-top high, twittering like children let out of school, and higher in the sky, the bee eaters and rollers, pretty little birds the size of starlings and with a peculiar flight, showed off their beauty as the sun picked up the electric blues and greens of their wings as they corkscrewed toward the ground: there was colour in heaven that day, and on earth. There was a myriad of wild flowers, every inch of ground was an excuse for them. I counted over twenty-four different ones within a few yards. The sides of the track were white rivers of marguerites, but every colour of the spectrum was represented. Blue, violet, orange and indigo, all were there, but predominant was the yellow of broom and the arterial red of poppies. They had bled everywhere, no field was without them. And in the air was the heavy burnt sugar smell of thyme.

I crossed a brook, clambered up the opposite muddy slope, turned left along another track, walked under the tall stone walls of a cemetery, paused as the smell of incense reached me, and went in through the open iron gates. In silence I looked at the memorials to Kardamena's dead. Behind glass-fronted niches on the white tombs, night lights and spent matches floated on saucers of oil. Each marble cross bore a plastic wreath and on each grave was a photograph of the departed. Dressed in their best they looked more stiff and unnatural in life than they were in death. An elderly widow, crow-black in her weeds, knelt in prayer, sending her orison to heaven in a puff of incense, and two more arrived as I left. I thought how good it was to be alive.

On the other side of the track in an olive grove a brown-and-white donkey, looking like a child's toy, blinked sleepily at me through a cloud of flies. I walked on past it, through the regimented trees and out into a field. At the end of it I picked and slid my way down the crumbling earth of a sudden slope, over tree roots laid bare by erosion and down to a little rocky stream set between banks of rhododendron, gorse and prickly pear. I followed its course, hop-scotching my way from rock to rock and side to side until eventually it became too deep and wide and I took to its muddy banks.

It was hot and still below the level of the fields. There was no breeze and the omnipresent humming of wild bees and a million other flying things increased the sense of airlessness. From beyond a bend in the river a frog croaked: it was answered by another. A third joined in, and then a fourth. And then another, and another and another until the reeds and bogs echoed to an Aristophanean chorus of hundreds. They stopped when they heard me coming, and panic-dived for safety with a plip! plip! plop! and joined the turtles below the surface of the slow-moving, pale-green water. A moment's silence as I passed and then: 'Kre-ok, Kre-ok,' called the chorus leader; and the din began again.

Either side of me the banks grew steeper and higher, the vegetation more dense, and half a mile later I pulled and panted my way through it, the dry spear grass slicing and pricking into my bare legs, and reached the top. I stood for a moment, cursing that I had not worn slacks and getting my bearings and my breath. Ahead of me were the hills; they were, I reckoned, another mile away. Two blue butterflies spiralled upward in a fluttering ariel love dance. I watched them, living their short lives to the full, and then set off again.

Now there was no path and the going grew harder. The scenery became wilder. I found myself going deeper and deeper into a land of gorges, crevices and cracks – a scene which I was to see again in the autumn. Then, after a five-months' baking in the sun it was like a lunar landscape, but that is when the whole countryside looks as though a sack of oatmeal has been spilled over it, and when it turns to a crock of gold in the evening sun – that is when the dust takes over and the donkeys seem to bray more rustily. There is an aridity about it, yet even then in sheltered places and where the beds of the mountain streams are not quite dry I found secret gardens thick with prickly pear and sward plants.

But on this May day the hills wore brown and green and there was pink and white on their upper slopes where the rains had washed the top soil off and uncovered fresh layers of the strata upon strata of untold millions of fossilized shells. All shapes and sizes were there and for a while I probed and prodded with a piece of stick, unearthing and pocketing miniature unicorn horns and scalloped fans, and then sat down among them. It was strange, I thought, as I ate my meal and looked around at the humps and peaks, that once they were all below the sea. I lit a pipe and stayed there for an hour, alone with my thoughts, looking at Kardamena below me in the distance and watching Turkey vanish in a growing haze; and then began my return journey.

I took a different route back and I arrived at the outskirts of the village at the opposite end from which I started, where the buildings were scattered and the main road joined the dirt track along the shore. By then it was late afternoon and Kardamena was waking from its siesta. Close to the beach and under an almirithra tree, those trees which grow in abundance where there is salt and on which the bees gorge themselves with nectar from the sweet-smelling, tiny, grey-white mimosa-like blossom, some children played on a home-made swing suspended from it. Others were busy with whips and wooden tops, and some little girls dressed in long skirts tossed stones into squares marked out in the dust. In the doorways of the buildings women sat, half listening to their transistors, gossiping and preparing vegetables for the evening meal; an old woman, bent with age and leaning upon a stick and carrying a plate of mash, emerged from a shack and called to her chickens with a 'Kree! Kree! Kree!' and a 'Kree! Kree! Kree!'; from the village road on my left an elderly cloth-capped man riding side-saddle and dozing upon a mule, rode slowly toward me, at peace with the world; and from the opposite direction, along the stony, dusty, bumpy road, their approach signalled by a clanking and squeaking, came the Gogs. On Yanni's bicycles.

Even at a hundred yards I could tell that they were unhappy Gogs. They rode uncertainly and were separated one from the other by several lengths. Magog was to the rear. Sitting bolt upright in her saddle, plainly discomforted by a cross-bar and looking neither to the left nor to the right but with her eyes set sternly on an indeterminate spot in the distance, she gave every impression that she had disowned her husband. This man, her expression said, is nothing to do with me – it is pure coincidence that we are travelling together; but it was Gog who excited my attention.

To say the least, his progress was erratic. Not only was he wobbling alarmingly but every two yards his knees pumped up and down like demented pistons as the chain divorced itself from the cogs of the flywheel. Then, as tension came back to the pedals, both rider and machine jerked forward convulsively with fresh momentum. I had no idea he was so foul-mouthed.

His advance was watched with considerable interest. The children on the swing left their rope and moved inland to get a better view, the little girls with the tops and stones picked up their toys and carried them to safety; and the bent old lady stopped saying 'Kree! Kree! Kree!' She gave a soft moan of apprehension, flung down her mash and hobbled behind a tree. One had the feeling that she had seen all this before and was taking no chances. Only the approaching mule and its rider seemed unaware of anything untoward.

Forty yards away Gog got a good run. Cogs and chain remained married, and by the time he was nearly upon us he had worked up quite a speed; and then it happened. As his front wheel hit a stone, his handlebars left their socket. For a split second Gog gazed at them in disbelief as he held them at arm's length and at eye level. 'Look!' he seemed to be saying, 'No hands,' and pedalled on, his ailing feet still going like clockwork. Ahead of him the mule, unable to believe the spectacle before it, stopped dead in its tracks then left the ground with all four feet simultaneously, shedding its rider and a quantity of dairy products as it did so. Five seconds later Gog embraced it warmly round the neck, appeared to say something in its ear, and together they disappeared quickly into a bakery. From within came shrieks and shouts and the sound of falling pastry. Then silence.

Outside, the mule's owner sat up in a pool of sheep's milk and inquired what had happened. A crowd of twenty enlightened him and assisted him to his feet. Another five stormed the bakery, retrieved the mule and dusted down Gog. Ten minutes later the inquest was over. The muleteer, fortified by an ouzo, remounted and departed, the children went back to their games and Gog and Magog wheeled the remains toward Yanni's. They were still there when I made my way toward my pension opposite.

'I'm so sorry,' I said.

They looked at me.

'This,' said Gog, 'is the Last Straw.'

'The Very Last,' said Magog.

'We shall Complain,' said Gog.

'Strongly,' said Magog.

'Of course,' said I, 'but at least you weren't hurt – were you?'

'No,' said Gog, 'I was not hurt, but,' and he paused, 'I have suffered a Major Disaster.' He paused again. 'I have,' he said in a voice which came from the grave, 'Broken My Truss.'

'Oh dear,' I said, and quickly crossed the street.

'Kalispera!' said Kosta from outside his shop, 'You hive hard a good dai?'

'Marvellous,' I said. 'And you?'

'Nau,' he said, 'I harve hard troubles with, how to sai – orthandopolus. You nau orthandopolus?' he inquired.

'No,' I said, 'I haven't met him.'

'Oche!' he said, 'naut him – *it*! It is like ponokefelos.'

'Ah,' I said, 'headache!'

'Ne!' said Kosta, 'but in the taithe – Ai harve the headaker-ina-the-taithe. But,' he said, watching the retreating figure of Gog whose gait resembled that of a superannuated equestrian, 'he, I think, has trouble with the bautums.'

'I think,' I said, 'that he has trouble with everything,' and went to my room.

Thankfully the water and the electricity had returned and I showered, changed, collected an ice cold bottle of retsina from Kosta's refrigerator, went on the roof and watched the sun go down over the dome of the little church, setting fire to the sky as it did so. For me at any rate it had been a splendid day and I gave thanks for it. Below me the street began to throb with chatter, and as the daylight faded so the lights came on and along the front the tavernas started to come to life.

Suddenly I felt hungry. I finished my wine, took the empty

left the ground with all four feet simultaneously

bottle back to Kosta in his shop and then walked down to Stelio's again.

Leon was still there and in precisely the same position as he was when I had seen him in the morning. Presumably he had moved, but there was no immediate indication that he had done so. He still held a coffee cup and he was still staring at the floor. 'Stelio!' he called unemotionally when he saw me, 'Stelio! – the Englishman is here again – the one with the pipe who arrived last night.'

From somewhere beyond a glass-fronted door there was the sound of hurried footsteps coming down the stairs and then into the room burst Stelio. He looked very drawn.

'Aa,' he said, and moved quickly toward me. 'My friend,' he said, speaking rapidly in English, 'it is good to see you! Your arrival was not very pleasant I think last night – so much wind, so much rain – sit down, please! Leon! – retsina, ne?' He was as relaxed as an E-string. 'Yes, my friend,' he continued, 'I am happy to see you because I have troubles, much troubles with your countrymen.' He jerked his head toward the open french window and the restaurant. There sat the Gogs eating their meal as though every mouthful was poisoned. Apart from a white-haired man in his late seventies, who was holding hands with a lady considerably his junior, they were the only ones to occupy the room.

'Yes,' said Stelio, pouring my retsina but taking none himself, 'much troubles. First the old man over there with the young woman. He is a nice good man and is here on his honeymoon. Five days he stays already and already you know what?' I shook my head. 'Two heart attacks,' said Stelio; and took a tablet. 'What will happen, I ask the God, in another week!' He clutched his stomach convulsively. 'Leon! – neró . . .!' And then, my friend,' he broke off to sip the water as it arrived, 'and then, the other two! Complain! complain! complain!

They have I think, no joy!' In the outer restaurant Gog choked on a fish bone. 'Excuse me,' said Stelio, and darted out to him with water. They engaged in earnest conversation. To their right the septuagenarian reluctantly disengaged himself from his bride and came through the doors with her.

He bowed toward me with old-fashioned courtesy. 'I hope,' he said, slowly, and throatily, 'you have a pleasant stay here. We have. Yes, the days have been er, very full really. Yes, very full; in fact, perfectly, er, er, perfect. Yes. Anyway I think it's time we were on our way up the er, er, wooden stairs. So goodnight to you and er,' and here he turned to Leon, 'Kali whatever it is to you.'

In a near-by taverna a fiddler started to play wild music and across the square I could see that people were dancing as the May Day celebrations got under way. I looked toward Stelio: he was still engaged with the Gogs.

I went over to the counter and ordered a swordfish steak and a salad. Across the way the music grew louder and more frenzied. Still Stelio did not come.

I fell upon the salad when it arrived. Halfway through the swordfish the Gogs entered the room as if following an imaginary bier with Stelio in attendance as chief mourner. They passed my table without a word.

'Goodnight,' said Stelio, administering the final rites as the cortège passed from view, 'goodnight.'

He stood, looking up the stairs until he heard their door close. Then, breathing a sigh of relief, he came across to me. 'They leave tomorrow,' he said, 'tomorrow morning they go to Kos – that will be better for them, I think; but I am sad they have been unhappy in Kardamena. And now, my friend, if you have finished – we go!' He raised his hands as I sought my wallet. 'Oche!' he said, 'No! No! No! Tonight you are my guest – ela!'

The fiddle music hit us as we went through the doors and grew in volume as we neared the taverna from which it came – where all Kardamena, it seemed, was dancing under the stars. Check-shirted and glassy-eyed like a hypnotized Grappelli, the fiddler scraped, on and on and on and on, from a straight-backed chair by the white-washed wall. And as the retsina bottles around him grew, faster and faster his fingers went, shorter and shorter the path of his bow and wilder and wilder the music came and wider and wider the circle of men as they joined in the island dance.

Hands on shoulders, shuffling feet, two steps forward one step back, two steps forward and one step back, then into the centre to show off their skill with a high-kicked leap and a limbo crouch and a smack of the hand on the sole of the shoe and an arrogant turn of the hips. And around them clapped and shouted and whistled the men and women on the fringe of the dance, tapping their feet in time to the tune as they sat at their tables with their bottles and awaiting their turn to take part. On and on the fiddler played, sweat stains growing and elbow going and then – abruptly, and in a long moan as he drew his bow full-length across the strings – the dance ended. 'Bravo! Bravo!' cried everyone, and the dancers collapsed into chairs.

It was a magnificent evening. For one reason and another the finer details of the latter part of it escape me. I think we stopped at two o'clock but it may well have been three. But I do remember that I was escorted back to Kosta's by Yanni the Bicycle on one arm and Dimitri the Taxi on the other. Attached to them were two Kostas, one Yiorgo, another Yanni; and a Yacobus. We were all singing. But we were not in tune.

CHAPTER III

The Drums of the Village

THE GOGS WERE not alone when they left for Kos the next morning. A disconsolate quorum, refugees from an unsuccessful villa party, stood near them in the square awaiting the arrival of taxis. As I drew close and halted to light my pipe, I heard one of them, a whey-faced young woman with a whining voice say: 'And if *that* wasn't enough, every time we used it the seat came off... yes, um – right off. What?... No, plarstic. Yes, yellow plarstic it was, yes. *And* it had a crack in it... yes a big crack – right in the front. What?... Well, no, not exactly, but it could have been ... yes, very painful ... yes, um. And another thing, too, Martin brought his Golden Shred but unfortunately there wasn't no toast for him to put it on ... No, not a scrap, no. *And* there wasn't no tea neither, no – I mean in Torremolinos we ...'

She sounded like an unoiled door hinge. I moved on, but she was still in need of lubrication when I returned a few minutes later and watched the taxis bear her, the Gogs and the marmalade-deprived Martin toward neon-lit and chromium-plated venues – the antitheses of Kardamena, which was not geared to tourist activities. It *was* difficult to get a nice cup of tea there, certain seating arrangements *were* suspect, and I was glad for their sakes that they had moved on to more compatible surroundings; but I would not have exchanged Kardamena for all the gold of Croesus.

It is a Dylan Thomas of a village, a Dodecanese Under Milk Wood where, as I found out within minutes, one end of the community will know accurately just how many bottles you consumed in the other, what you had for supper, what you paid for it and a precise intelligence of the enormities you committed afterwards.

'Ah, Yanni! You drink seven bottles last night with Vasili and dance on Michaelis's table – ne? Ha! Ha! bravo! bravo!'

Incidentally, for the sake of my reputation and despite the fact that Kardamena does contain more ardent disciples of Bacchus than are to be found in many other islands, retsina is marketed in very small bottles and, moreover, one is seldom allowed to drink alone. Nevertheless the number of empties on one's table is noted keenly by the cognoscenti and used as a barometer for evaluating one's current form.

Without doubt the village has the finest bush telegraph system in the world – nothing goes unnoticed: and, like the Welsh, they are a dramatic people in Kardamena. No happening, however small, is allowed to remain unembroidered. They thrive on drama, and without it they would die. Not that they are often left long without material – nearly every day something of note happens in the village. The Gogs had taken the stage on Sunday, two cars embraced the day they left, there was a fight on the Wednesday and another on Thursday; and a dead cow was washed up on a beach on the Friday. I discovered it on one of my walks and reported it to Yanni and Yacobus the agricultural policemen in the evening over supper.

'A dead *cow*?' said Yanni, lowering his glass.

'A *dead* cow?' said Yacobus, doing likewise.

'Yes,' I said, 'a dead cow.'

'How dead?' said Yanni.

'Very dead,' I said.

'Does it stink?' said Yacobus.

'It smells,' I said.

'Then soon it will stink,' said Yanni, 'and when it stinks the flies will come.'

'And with the flies,' said Yacobus, entering into the spirit of things, 'there will be disease!'

'And deaths,' said Yanni, thinking no doubt of what happened to Thebes and bringing down the curtain, 'many, many deaths.'

'We are,' said Yacobus, 'glad that you have told us – we will take action!'

'Immediate action!' said Yanni, banging his glass on the table. 'Tomorrow,' said Yacobus, refilling it.

'Yes,' said Yanni, 'tomorrow morning, at daybreak, we will go to the cow.'

'With our tractor –'

'And our spades –'

'And tow it away –'

'And dig a hole –'

'A large, deep hole –'

'And bury it.'

'And bury it!' said Yacobus conclusively.

They turned to me and beamed. 'Leave it to us!' they said.

It was still there when I left five days later and its skull grinned at me when I returned in the autumn. However, useful though that incident was in spurring the inherent imagination and creative skills of Yanni and Yacobus it was nothing compared with the stimulus afforded to the many on the following day.

At about seven o'clock the next morning I leant over the

balcony of my room, enjoying the first pipe of the day, and watching life. There was not much to see at that hour. Yanni the Bicycle was on duty performing an early autopsy; further down the street Yanni the Barber was having a pre-breakfast and two-handed scratch at his stomach as he watched Sylvi unwind the striped awning outside her shop, and two old men with grizzled faces sat against the wall of the taverna next door. One was drinking coffee, and the other was exploring his nose. Opposite, and unnoticed by Yanni the Bicycle, a mongrel dog with a curly tail and a lolling tongue trotted from around a corner, anointed a spare wheel and bounced away with a happy smile. It was all very peaceful. And then, unexpectedly, the calm was shattered.

From the doorway, twenty feet below me, a young English woman, whom I knew to be a spinster and with impeccable credentials, walked uncertainly into the centre of the street, swayed twice, and then measured her length with a thud which must have been heard in Turkey.

It was just what Kardamena needed. Yanni took off in a shower of spokes and inner tubing, the index finger of the octogenerian went through his head and his companion suffered total immersion in his own coffee. And from out of the shops and tavernas and houses, people came running like hens toward corn. From all directions they came and by the time I had rushed down the stairs and reached the ringside the girl had been placed in a chair and was the centre of a two-deep circle of babbling samaritans.

'Fetch the doctor, fetch the –'

'No! No! No! he is no good, not yet, I saw him last night – bring some ouzo!'

'Ah, Dimitri, you are right! Of course, of course, the ouzo, that is what she needs – Kosta, bring some ouzo, with ouzo she will be all right, I think?'

'But perhaps she does not like the ouzo?'

'Nonsense, everybody likes the ouzo!'

'But perhaps she –'

'Well pour it over her head, rub it in her hair!'

'Oche – open it under her nose, that will wake her up.'

'But what is the matter?'

'Thenkatalava! I was mending Yiorgo's bicycle and –'

'Perhaps she is dying!'

'True! Perhaps she is!'

'Perhaps already she is dead! Perhaps –'

On the periphery a very large lady with a bristly chin folded her arms and in a voice which carried loud and clear above the hubbub said: 'Perhaps it is an affair of the child! Whenever young women faint before breakfast it is because of a child!'

It was a great conversation stopper.

'True?' asked the district nurse manqué, looking around her for support from the other senior members of the mother's union who were present. 'True?'

'Ah yes,' they said, 'very true. Yes we all fainted before breakfast, yes; sometimes twice.'

At that moment the centre of attention regained consciousness. To a relieved chorus of 'Aaah! She breathes! She breathes! Bravo! Bravo!' she fluttered her eyes, crossed them once and shook her head.

'Oh dear!' she said. 'Oh! Oh Golly!' And everyone clapped.

But the bristly lady did more than that. Elbowing her way to the front and pointing a benevolent finger in the direction of the stricken one's tummy she beamed and inquired in English: 'Preeg-noont-yes? Ba-be! You have ba-be?'

'Oh, gosh,' said the girl turning an even worse colour, 'oh, no, no, no! No, nothing like that! Really, honestly! Actually I think it's the sun. You know, a touch of er, helios!'

I was not sufficiently proficient in Greek to know the

equivalent of 'Tell that to the marines' but the bristly lady's expression implied that there was one.

'Yes,' she said, patting the girl on the cheek, 'of course – the sun!'

'Ah, yes!' chorused the gallery, 'of course – the sun!', and drifted away pondering on the strange euphemisms employed by the English.

Nobody ever did find out for certain what the cause was because she left three days later, for Cheltenham I suspect, but the conjecture kept the drums beating for days.

I took her to her room. She was all right but I suggested that she lay down on her bed. As she did so, Kosta and his wife, Anastasia, arrived. She carried a basin of ice and a tea towel, and he carried a bucket.

'In case of the bruises and the headache,' said Anastasia, emptying a generous amount of ice into the tea towel and putting it on the girl's head.

'And,' said Kosta, placing the bucket beside her, 'in case of the sicks!'

'What sweet people,' said the girl as I left her.

'Yes,' I said, 'they are – all of them.'

That vignette demonstrated the love and manufacture of high drama; but it also endorsed what I had found out already; it is not everywhere that folk will run toward a mishap to give help. But one does not have to be long in Kardamena to discover what a closely knit community it is.

Everyone knows everybody and everyone appears, however distantly, to be related: there was, for instance, it seemed to me, a uni-kit nose in Kardamena. And it is a village in which within a very short while one realizes that one side of the street has married the other. Even the dogs bear the same markings. Chocolate and white, they look like pointers gone wrong. I met them everywhere, eyeing the cats who also share a common ancestry – patently at one time an orange tom of great age and immense vigour had roamed those streets.

Kardamena is not without blemish: no community is and it is no exception. Hate and jealousy, envy and avarice breed there as they do in any village and some cancers run deeper than they would in England. The X's do not talk to the Y's, and never will. Generations past the daughter of one family was jilted by the other's son; and the cold war will continue until the end of time. Hurt pride and broken marriage settlements are not easily forgotten or forgiven although each Sunday the little church is filled with temporary penitents.

I attended a service there on the Sunday morning a week after my arrival and saw Kardamena at worship. I went in through the front entrance and stopped hesitantly. From inside came the sound of men's voices raised in harmony, and the smell of incense hit me as I waited behind two women who bought candles from a reception committee in charge of a huge plate filled with drachmae. For a split second the eyebrows of the keepers of the plate went up as they saw me and then – 'Yasas Yanni! Yasas! Yasas!' – Ela!', and they escorted me in. I had seen them in the village but I had not met them; but they knew me by name.

As I went in, the heads in the rear rows turned toward me and elbows worked overtime as the news was passed on, nudge by nudge, whisper by whisper and row by row until I reached my seat. 'Yasas!' said the man next to me.

The church was nearly full. On one side were the women, their heads shawl-covered, and on the other were the men, clean shaven and stiff in their best. Standing, or sitting on wooden chairs, they crossed and recrossed themselves in the name of Christ as, from a lectern in the front Yanni the Barber, pink and tenor-high and leading his male choir of three, responded unaccompanied to the bass of the Baker opposite as they sang together in praise of God, their faces quivering to produce their vibratos. On and on they sang, filling the church with glorious sound as page after page of the great books of prayer were turned by their helpers. There was never a silence, and in the body of the church there was always movement as people came and went.

Along the sides of the church sat the elders of the village, perched high in wooden stalls, their arms resting on high supports. Never glancing to the right nor to the left and never moving unless to cross themselves or clean their ears – a pursuit which seemed to be a popular Sabbath occupation – they leaned forward intently, staring fixedly toward the altar. They looked like stone-carved griffins or Cappo di Monte figures.

From time to time the papa appeared in splendid vestments and, attended by unrobed acolytes, intoning the litany and blessing the congregation he toured the church, waving his censer toward us. At one point he was overcome with a paroxysm of coughing.

'Too many cigarettes,' said the man next to me, 'he smokes forty a day – this always happens.' 'Yes,' said the man in front of me, half turning as he made the sign of the cross, 'he should give it up.' The papas recovered, returned red-eyed to the privacy of the sanctuary and blew his nose vigorously.

A party of thirty or forty little girls, cotton fresh in pinks and whites and floral dresses, rustled in like a spring breeze and made their way to the front and gathered around Yanni's lectern; and an equal number of little boys, all newly scrubbed and smelling of soap, did similarly on my side but with less delicate tread. The papas appeared again, had another coughing fit, blessed the new arrivals, retired, and a few minutes later two painted screens moved by unseen hands came jerkily together in front of the altar. The service was over. There was a con-

certed rush to grab pieces of bread – a gift from the papas –
from a large wicker basket placed near the side door, and then
everyone streamed out; but not before nearly every male in
the church had said good morning to me and shaken me by
the hand. I had been greeted with curiosity and smiles when I
arrived, but I left feeling doubly warmed and welcomed: I had
become part of a family.

I pondered on that as I walked slowly to Sylvi's for my
yoghurt. I tried hard to recall when a similar welcome had
been given to me in the past when I had visited a strange church
in my own country. Unfortunately I could not. We may not
clean our ears with matchsticks during the Creed in rural
England but we are not quick to open our hearts to strangers.

'Ah!' said Kosta, when I returned to pick up my knapsack
from my room, 'so you harve bane to the churcha, ne? And
you crause yourself the prauper why! From right to left, ne?
Bravo! You har the gooda boy! And becaws you har the gooda
boy you gau to Haiven, ne? But me,' he said, making a spot
confession, 'I ham the bada boy! I do not gau to the churcha
todai but,' he concluded triumphantly, 'I still gau to the Haiven
becaws Hi ham the friend of the papas! I give him – cigarettes!'

Ten minutes later I saw Stelio. 'Did you enjoy the church?'
he asked.

'Very much,' I said, 'but I didn't see you there.'

'Oche!' he said, 'I was not there; but my cousin Yanni was.
Also Leon. Also my wife. For myself,' he continued, 'I do not
believe in the God. Also I think the priests have too much power
and too much money. And Yanni,' he said reprovingly, 'to
put thirty drachmae in the plate *and* without taking a candle
. . . po! po! po! po! po!'

He went on his agnostic way shaking his head and leaving
me to muse, not only on the fresh evidence of the excellence of
Kardamena's intelligence network, but on Kosta's revelation

that although the road to Hell is paved with good intentions
the route to Heaven is lined with nicotine. However, despite
Stelio's analysis of the priesthood the papas had not given me
the impression of power-crazed opulence, even when dressed
in his official robes, and I found it even harder to believe in
the portrait when I came face to face with him in the street
in the late afternoon. What I did see was a small, rather tatty
man with an abundance of grey beard and, as far as I could
determine through the hair, a kind face with twinkling grey
eyes. His black robes were badly in need of dry cleaning and
his general appearance was that of a shopsoiled Father Christmas
in mourning.

'Heréte!' he said, when he recognized me, 'Greetings! It
was good to see you in church this morning! But could you
understand?'

'About half,' I said.

'Never mind,' he said, patting my arm, 'never mind! You
understand half but you get all the blessings, ne?' He laughed
wheezily and fumbled under his robes for a cigarette. 'You will
come again to Kardamena?'

'Yes,' I said, 'I think so – many times. I shall try to return
in the autumn but especially I should like to spend Easter
here.'

'Ah yes, my friend,' he said, accepting a light from me, 'that
is the time – especially for the Church! That is when we say
"Christos Anesti! Christos Anesti! – Christ is risen!" '

'I know,' I said, 'I know: but tell me – if I come to church at
Easter, will you be able to give me Communion?'

'But of course,' he said, 'why not? We are one Church are
we not? You are a Protestant, ne?' I nodded. 'Then there is no
trouble,' he said.

He paused to draw on his cigarette. 'Only one, small, small
problem: you will have to go to the Bishop in Kos to get his

permission in writing for me to give you Communion but er, there is no worry.'

'I see,' I said, 'but it has to be done through the Bishop?'

'Oh yes,' he said, inhaling again, 'yes. Everything has to be done through the Bishop. In fact, my friend, in Greece we have a saying, and it is this: in life *we* are under the *bishops*, but in death –' and here his eyes twinkled wickedly and he pointed downward, '*they* are under *us*. Yasas!' And off he went, wheezing at his own irony. He was a nice little man who smelt strongly of incense and tobacco smoke, and I enjoyed his humour; and indirectly I was remined of him by references to his church at intervals during the evening.

At the taverna which I used more than most I had five bottles of retsina that night; but I only bought one. One was sent across to me by a wart-laden gentleman who had sung in the choir, the second came from the husband of the stout lady I had seen ringing the bell, and the remaining two bottles were donated by the officer-in-charge of the offertory plate. The unworthy thought did cross my mind that with regard to the gifts of the latter there might be a connection between his double generosity and my donation of thirty drachmae, but I dismissed it quickly. The Lord, I remembered, often moves in mysterious ways and it was not for me to question His servants; but I came to know of the influence of the Church in another way that night.

The taverna was owned by Kosta's brother Michaelis. It was small, not too clean and the speed of service left much to be desired. Agreed, Michaelis – a great believer in Time and Motion – did try to make amends for the interval between order and delivery by hurling the entire meal on the table together complete with knife and fork, but as he permanently wore dark glasses it was not unusual for a high proportion of it to go on the floor. From there it was retrieved, given a brisk

wipe over, and replaced. However, despite its somewhat un-
orthodox presentation the food was good and the taverna was
always well patronized by locals and national servicemen
from the near-by garrison.

That night was no exception; by half past eight the place was
packed with them. And as soldiers do all over the world, they
drank and they sang. And the more they drank the more they
sang and for two hours and more Michaelis's taverna echoed
with songs of the Dodecanese and the Cyclades and of Northern
Greece and Crete. Folk songs, love songs and songs of praise,
revolutionary songs by Theodorakis, songs of the sponge-
fishers of Kalymnos – all were sung, and in voices as deep and
as dark as a pit. But whatever they sang one could detect the
early training that all had had in Greek liturgical singing – the
ability to sustain and control a note. Toward eleven o'clock,
when the retsina had taken control, the discipline did waver a
little and the sound was more like that of a rugby club
returning after a victory, but earlier they were superb.

As the soldiers left en masse for their transport the husband of
Poppi, the overweight campanologist, rose with some difficulty
from his seat. He was a stocky man in his early sixties with
close-cropped grey hair and a clipped moustache. His face, the
colour of mahogany, was lined like a relief map of the
Irrawaddy, and without being unkind, in my mind's eye I saw
him on top of a barrel-organ with a little red hat and a collect-
ing tin. He was a fisherman and ex-sailor and one of the world's
great givers. His name was Vasili and we were destined to
become firm friends.

After some seconds of concentrated effort he achieved an
upright position and gazed at me fondly.

'You,' he said, swaying slightly, 'went to church! Went to
church.' He repeated the phrase several times. 'And so did my
wife. Her name is ... is.' His eyes dulled then brightened again

with enlightenment, 'Ne! Poppi! She pulls the bell.' He tugged slowly at an imaginary rope somewhere above his head. 'Every day! But me?' He closed his eyes and his brows went up in an unspoken negative. 'I did not go to church. You see,' he said, confidentially and steadying himself with my shoulder, 'I have no liver!'

'No liver?' I said.

'No liver!' he repeated firmly, 'and no kidneys!'

I looked at him incredulously. 'Are you sure?' I said.

He staggered from me aghast and affronted. 'Am I sure?' he repeated, 'look!' And he hauled up two pullovers, a shirt, and a woollen vest to expose his stomach.

'Yes!' he said dramatically, and pointed to a gall bladder scar which appeared to have been made by a local butcher, '*THEY ALL CAME OUT OF THERE!* And that,' he said, lowering the layers but omitting to tuck them in, 'is why I may die tomorrow. But,' he added, momentarily forgetful of time and his imminent death, 'I shall go to church at Easter.'

Slowly we walked outside. A star shone brightly at the end of the street. Vasili looked at it for some time and eventually got it in focus.

'It will be a fine day tomorrow,' he said. 'Kalinichta.'

'Kalinichta,' I said, 'and thank you for the wine.'

'Tipota,' he said – 'don't mention it: you must eat with us before you go.' And walked unsteadily away. For a man deprived of his most vital organs he made remarkable progress.

Vasili may have been morose and hypochondriacal in his cups, but drunk or sober he was, and still is, a good weather forecaster. The next day was fine and I spent much of it breaking new ground.

I walked out of the village from the opposite end to the square and along the winding dusty track which ran parallel to

'*They all came out of there!*'

the beaches. They were speckled with sparkling black particles washed in from the volcanic island of Niceros across the way and littered with driftwood and bleached tree stumps. There was a slight breeze blowing inland and it skimmed the surface of the sea making it look like velvet brushed the wrong way.

I saw one person on the early part of my journey. An elderly man, stark naked and presumably a yoga enthusiast, was standing on his head in the middle of an otherwise deserted beach. As I passed him, the lines of Carroll's 'Aged, Aged Man' went through my head and I found myself saying aloud, 'and yet you incessantly stand on your head – do you think at your age it is right?' But there was no one to hear me and I carried on, lost in my thoughts. Past a monumental rubbish dump of smouldering debris and tin cans, past the dead cow, now twice as large as life and, as the breeze told me, doing nicely, past herds and flocks of sheep and goats, their bells clanking and jingling in different keys as they grazed on the shrub-covered slopes and on and on until I had neither man nor beast for company. And there, in blissful solitude, I had a swim in the clear blue waters, warm as a bath, and then sat down under an almirithra tree and watched the newly washed sand begin to shine brighter and brighter as a steamed-up mirror does as it clears; and fell asleep.

It was about three o'clock when I started on the two-hour trek back. Four hundred yards offshore a fishing boat chugged its way sleepily toward Kardamena. The figure at the helm waved to me. It was Vasili, liver- and kidney-less, but now fully recovered from his extravagances of the night before. He bent forward in the boat and then stood up holding a large fish.

'Kala ! – ne?' he called across the water.

'Poli kala!' I shouted back. 'Very good. Bravo!' He roared with laughter, waved again with his free hand, and chugged on.

He reminded me very much of Hemingway's 'Old Man and the Sea', and when I came to know him better I told him so. 'Ah!' he said, 'I know that book, that story of the old man and the fish. Ne! Seven years ago, in Athens, I saw a boy with it in Youlis Street. It had a fish on the coloured cover, a fine fish. So I stopped him, read a few pages of the book and bought it from him. Sosta! True – I have it still.' Vasili was full of surprises.

I watched him disappear around Dead Cow point and walked on steadily. Two crows flew over me laughing coarsely as they told each other risqué stories. 'Do you know that ravens do it on the wing – Caw! Caw! Caw! Caw! Caw!' On they flew, keeping vulgar station with each other and then swooped down to join others on the rubbish dump with its eternal smoke. Further on the yoga enthusiast was still at it, no longer on his head but attempting to Open The Lotus. To judge from his expression he was using the wrong key; and to judge from the colour of his back, which was bright red, his meditations on the following day would be made on his stomach. I left him behind, happy with his masochism, and ten minutes later entered the village.

I did not approach it by the road but by way of the beach, and then, clambering over the stones which marked the end of the concrete front, I started to walk under a newly thatched verandah roof which extended from the front of a freshly white-washed building.

It had a grilled window and the door was a quarter open. Through it came the unmistakable smell of incense. I did not know it but I was about to be blessed for the second time in two days. As I drew level with the door and paused to have a sniff, it opened a little wider. A voice from within said: 'Pst! Pst! Yanni! Ela! Peraste! Peraste!', and before I knew what had happened I had been yanked inside and into a cloud of incense. I was totally unprepared for the scene before me.

Standing in a row in front of the counter of the taverna – for that is what it was – their hands clasped before them, were the friends and relatives of the owners, Yiorgo and Dimitri. Yacobus was there, so was his colleague Yanni, and so was the Gog-struck muleteer. Next to him was the offertory plate man, and to his left, a trio of plump ladies.

Against the wall facing them, and to the right of the door, a small table had been turned into an altar. Upon it was a tiny cross, a bowl of rose-water and some flowers. In front of it and bending from the waist were the brothers Yiorgo, and Dimitri. Behind them, and in full cry, was the papas. When I made my entrance he was intoning some prayers which, in the main, seemed to be directed toward Yiorgo and Dimitri. Whether they heard them or not is debatable as they were huddled together with their heads covered by a thick communal cloth and appeared to be breathing with difficulty : Yiorgo I remember was particularly stentorian and showed signs of restlessness under the blanket, but all was well. With a quick movement which would have done credit to a trainee matador, the papas removed the covering with a swirl, toured the entire establishment with his censer working overtime – an action which increased the respiratory difficulties of everyone present – and repeated the procedure with rose-water. This he flung over everything with great abandon, and then blessed us individually and by name. That finished, he sat down, lit a cigarette, and we all drank warm champagne under a sodden poster of a chimpanzee who, despite its soaking, continued to grin and extol the virtues of tea.

It was a happy occasion and I felt privileged to have been invited to the blessing, albeit at short notice. The papas said how nice it was to see me again, I reminded Yacobus and Yanni of the dead cow, Yiorgo and Dimitri said that they hoped that

I would be at their grand opening of their taverna that night, and I said that I should be. And I was.

It was a memorable evening. I arrived quite early, but even then the place was packed. Vasili was there, so were Yacobus and Yanni, so was Kosta, so was Yanni the Bicycle – in fact it seemed to me that only the bedridden and breast-fed of Kardamena were absent. Overhead, chains of fairy lights twinkled from the verandah roof, three ancient fiddlers were scraping away for dear life, and everyone was eating and drinking as if there were no tomorrow. Clearly the evening was going to be a success.

As I remember there was only one hitch in the proceedings: each time somebody went to the loo, which on average was once every five minutes, the lights went out. This may have been coincidence, but knowing the shortcomings of Greek plumbers and electricians I doubted it; and the green flash which lit the interior of the cubicle when the chain was pulled served to reinforce my suspicions. However, be that as it may, the interferences were a little distracting because whenever we were plunged into darkness there was a scream of anguish from the aged trio of fiddlers as one or another of them was impaled in the ear by his companion's bow and the music came to a halt.

Despite these unscheduled diversions Yiorgo and Dimitri were obviously delighted with the way things were going – they rushed from table to table answering the cries of the hungry and thirsty and waited upon them with unbounded enthusiasm. From time to time they nodded appreciatively toward the papas who sat smiling benignly through a permanent cloud of cigarette smoke. Plainly his earlier efforts were being rewarded: if ever I had doubt of the efficacy of prayer it was removed then; and I said as much to Vasili who was sitting next to me. 'My goodness,' I said, 'the papas's prayers have been answered –

there are many people here! This is good business for Yiorgo and Dimitri!'

'Ah, yes,' he said, 'yes, yes. Yes, the power of the priest is very great. And God,' he said, crossing himself, 'is very good – there are many people here. But my friend we must not forget one thing.' He paused. 'Tonight,' he said, 'the food is free.'

One of the many things which draw me to the Greek islander is his sense of irony and his ability to mix the spiritual with the material: somehow his feet are always on the ground.

Time rushed from me in the next two days.

On the Wednesday before I left I climbed the hills again to the mediaeval castle I could see from Kosta's. It was near a village called Antimachia and was one of the long chain of fortifications left by the Crusaders on their marches across Europe to the Holy land.

I leaned over the battlements and looked down at Kardamena bathed in the afternoon sunlight. It was not picturesque in the picture postcard sense; but I did not see buildings. I saw the soul of the village – a community which in eleven days had shown me warmth, hospitality and friendship, and to which I felt I belonged; and then and there I resolved to return to it.

I turned my back on the panorama, walked out of the ruins and through the wild crocus which sprinkled them, and on to the cart-track leading to the main road to Kardamena. Near the junction a party of soldiers sat and lazed outside their depôt. I recognized some as the ones who had sung in Michaelis's on Sunday and called out to them as I passed.

'Ya!' they chorused in return. It was like the rumbling of falling rocks.

That evening was spent in saying goodbye, and at four o'clock the next morning I stood near Kosta's waiting for Dimitri to take me to Kos and to the ferry. In the western sky the swirling star-studded body of the Scorpion was beginning to pale and dip its head toward the horizon, and to the east Venus glared like an arc lamp as it heralded the dawn.

I said goodbye to Dimitri on the quayside, boarded the ferry and watched the dawn break and the sun rise as we pulled away for Rhodes.

As I leaned over the rails I was joined by the elderly honeymooner. He had lost a good deal of weight since I last saw him. 'What a splendid place,' he said, 'don't you think?' I nodded. 'And such decent people – don't you think?' I nodded a second time. 'All the same,' he said, 'it'll be nice to get a good cup of tea again. Don't you think? . . .'

CHAPTER IV

Autumn, Spring and Dispensation

I RETURNED TO Kardamena during the last week in September and I did not like what I saw. The village had been 'discovered' during the peak summer months and looked like the landscape – tired and dusty. By the time I arrived the numbers of tourists had thinned considerably, and three weeks later, save for myself, there were no visitors. But those first two weeks . . .

For half a mile or more, one- and two-person tents littered the speckled beaches and washing hung from the almirithra trees. During the day the incumbents, mostly unkempt young Germans and Americans with a smattering of British and other nationals, sprawled naked around their encampments strumming guitars and showing scant regard for the locals. In the evening they invaded the village, scrounging and spending little. Michaelis's was always full of them. Night after night they sat there, some staring through cannabis-glazed eyes and all occasionally addressing each other as 'Man', regardless of sex. In many cases that was difficult to determine; but the whores among them found favour with the soldiers and other unattached males, both indigenous and migratory.

At the other end of the village Stelio's hotel was still full of well-behaved and predominantly middle-aged and middle-class British. They did not address each other as 'Man' and although I once heard the form 'squire' used by a man who not infrequently told people that he travelled in pies, 'old man', 'old boy' and 'my dear' seemed to be used more often than not.

'Have another noggin, old man?' 'No thanks, old man, touch of the gyppos today.' 'Spot of beach-bashing this morning, old man?' 'Rather! nothing like it, old boy.' 'My dear, my bed collapsed and I wasn't even cavorting on it.' 'My dear, she had *all* her clothes *orf*'; and, 'My dear, I know she *says* she's his wife, but –'

All in all they presented the aura of a suburban tennis club in the Home Counties having an At Home; and they did what all good Britons do abroad – they set up a colony which within no time at all was imbued with all the mystique and mystery of the English class system.

Understandably and very properly they did not mix with the locals, unless to patronize their shops; understandably and very properly none attempted to speak Greek; and understandably and very properly they were very proper. True, from time to time Homer not only nodded but actually dropped off and I was fortunate enough to be privy to one of these rare spectacles. That was a night when, to the astonishment of everyone, a fat lady from Bradford kicked off her shoes, clambered with some difficulty upon a table, announced to all and sundry that she had 'the hots on Stelio' and then instructed her husband to go away and have an unnatural and impossible relationship with himself; but such lapses from grace were rare in Stelio's.

In the centre of the village and between the two social extremes the pensions were crowded with Germans and Swedes, Dutch and English, and one or two Australians. By night they crowded the tavernas and by day most of them lay on the beaches. The English and the Dutch retained a modicum of modesty and concern for local feelings. The Germans arrogantly bared their buttocks to the sun within sight of the tavernas.

On my third day back Vasili took me out in his boat and together we chugged along the coast. 'Look!' he shouted over the engine noise, and pointed to the stretched-out bodies on the shore. 'It is like a butcher's shop! But that is nothing! In July and August they were like sausages – bare sausages. Two came to my house. With a little child. They woke me up. In the morning. They had nowhere to sleep. And the child was hungry.'

'What did you do?' I shouted.

He shrugged his shoulders. 'What can one do? They were in trouble. And there was the child. I gave them my bed. But it is not right, Yanni. It is not right. Sosta?'

'Sosta!' I said, 'but they are not all like that.'

'Oche!' he said, 'there are good ones, of course. Many good ones. We welcome them. But the bad ones, the long-haired ones who look like girls and the girls who look like men – they bring disease and drugs. I have seen it. And it is not good for Kardamena.'

We sailed on. Kardamena, I thought, was materially richer than it had been, but, like Vasili, I wondered if the village had considered the cost it was going to pay.

When I got back to Kosta's, from the room below me English pop music blared out from a cassette player, its cacophony matched by another from the pension opposite. In the street a pink man with his nose swathed in lint and sticking plaster was holding forth about the visit he had made that day to the volcanic crater on Niceros.

'Strewth!' he said to an enthralled audience of one, 'it was bleeding 'ot I tell yer – me shoes melted!'

'They never,' said his listener, disbelievingly.

'They did,' said the pink one, 'melted! That's what they done. Bubbled up and melted. Ask Ethel.'

'Cor,' said his audience, 'makes yer think, don't it?'

'It does,' said the pink man, 'they oughter tell yer that, yer know – that yer shoes melt when yer stand on larva. There should be notices an' that–knowwotamin? "This larva is 'ot" – in English, so everyone can unnerstan.' He sucked his teeth reflectively. 'An' Ethel stinks of sulphur an' all.'

And so the human traffic came and went. A daily coach from Kos unloaded its cargo at Stelio's from where, after eating, the passengers promenaded through the main street or along the beaches and then departed still heavy with swordfish and souvlaki.

In the village the numbers gradually diminished as the pleased and disgruntled left for home, some to return and others to write letters of spurious complaint to their travel agents until at the end of the fortnight only a handful remained. It was selfish of me but I rejoiced that soon, once again, I should be able to sit at a table and be joined by Michaelis, no longer run off his feet, or talk with Kosta about the day or have an un-interrupted drink with Stelio and, above all, that again I should be able to stroll alone along the beaches. And it was those thoughts which preoccupied me as I set out to walk along them.

I remember the day well. There were no tents that I could see. The encampments had gone and only scattered papers, a torn string vest fluttering from a bush, and piles of blackened stones marking the cooking fires of the departed hippy population showed that they had been there. A solitary goat chewed experimentally on a discarded gum shoe; but I did not remain alone for long.

I had not gone far from the village when four piglets who

shared a roadside hovel with a mule and half a dozen hysterical hens scampered out of their front door and joined me. They were pink, rather sweet and reminded me of the sugar pigs of my childhood. I have no idea why they joined me. Maybe they were bored, or perhaps they had noticed that I was eating an apple, but join me they did and nothing would persuade them to go home. So on we went, munching and grunting respectively and, as one does with piglets, occasionally passing the time of day. When I stopped, they stopped and when I continued they did also.

We covered a quarter of a mile in this manner and were enjoying each other's company hugely when suddenly I saw what I did not wish to see. Pitched quite close to the track was a last remaining tent. It was one of the two-person variety and obviously occupied; from within came the sound of heavy breathing. There was also a good deal of movement.

Very slowly my friends and I approached it, and then halted.

I looked at it with loathing and the piglets gathered around me twitching their noses inquisitively.

What I did next was unworthy; but I could not help myself – I had become possessive about the beach. I took my apple core and showed it to Piglet One. He sniffed at it appreciatively and started to salivate; and so did the others. Then, very carefully and with, I am convinced, Divine Guidance, I lobbed it toward the tent. Together we watched it roll under the side flap. It did exactly what I wanted it to do; and so did my little pink friends.

Quietly they bunched nearer and nearer to the moving canvas until they were within sniffing distance. Piglet One halted, looked around at the rest and back-pedalled. Piglet Two took over and did similarly; so did Piglet Three. There was a brief conference and then once more Piglet One went to the fore. Urged on by his brothers he squared his shoulders, lowered his head, and with nostrils working overtime he stuck it under the flap; and blew.

Whether the moan which came from within was one of ecstasy or horror was difficult to determine, but the breathing stopped, and so did the movement. There was a moment of silence and then the quiet of the beach was shattered by a piercing scream, and the tent collapsed. I did not wait to see what happened next. Nor did the piglets. Together we turned tail and fled to our respective homes; but the tent was not there the following day.

As an after-dinner topic the episode was a great success. It went down well in Michaelis's that evening and continued to do so for the remainder of my stay, although by the time I left the original account had been so embroidered by each narrator that I found it hard to recognize the original. As I have said, the Greeks are splendid tellers of stories and never allow veracity to spoil a good tale.

That day was almost the last with unbroken sun. From then on each morning brought more and more cloud as October made way for November. It was still mild but strong winds raised the dust and plucked the litter from the plastic trash baskets hanging on the walls. They lashed the sea and rocked the fishing boats in the harbour, moaned and sighed through the telegraph wires festooning the street and rattled the wooden shutters of the houses. Winter was not far from Kardamena. Sylvi put away her green and orange awning and took her chairs inside. Vasili added a third pullover to his other two and Kosta moved his desk in his shop to the lee of the door and donned a beret.

'Kala himona!' they said as I left for the airport, 'Good winter!' and settled down to tot up the season's takings and to play cards behind closed doors.

I lobbed it toward the tent

When I next saw them it was Easter and the days were blue and white again and the countryside dressed for spring.

Easter! It is the Festival of Festivals in Greece. The date for the celebration of it by the Greek Orthodox Church is at variance with ours, and in 1978 Easter Day fell upon April 30th, five weeks or so after ours. But that is not the only difference: there the religious significance of the occasion is observed much more strictly than in Britain.

I arrived two days before the solemn week leading to Easter Day and to a welcome which stirred my heart. There were embraces all round in the middle of the street and bottles appeared as if by magic. Then after a three-hours' sleep and a bear-hugged tour of the village to say 'Hallo' I supped in Michaelis's off six large fish supplied by Vasili, skorthia – a splendid way of using up old bread and garlic – a huge salad and five bottles of retsina.

After my fourth fish I pushed my plate away. Vasili looked at me inquiringly.

'What is the matter?' he asked, 'is it not good?'

'Yes,' I said, 'it is very good but I have had enough.'

'Oche!' he said, spearing the fifth and putting it on my plate, 'you must eat! You must eat all you can! Sosta?' he inquired of the rest of the table, 'true?'

'Sosta,' they chorused, 'you must eat all you can!'

'But why?' I asked.

'Because Yanni,' said Vasili soulfully, 'from Monday until Easter Day you cannot eat fish.'

'Nor meat,' said Michaelis, annexing the sixth mullet and tearing it in half.

'Nor eggs,' said Yanni the Bicycle, falling on the remainder and continuing the recital of the diet sheet for the coming week through a mouthful of bones, 'nor eggs, milk, cheese, yoghurt – nothing that come from an animal.'

'Nothing!' endorsed Michaelis, 'that is the custom.'

There was silence to allow me to digest these hard facts of life and for Yanni to fillet his teeth while I stared hard at the table. I was a little dismayed. I was anxious to take part in all their Easter celebrations but, having enforced my own period of self-denial during our Lent five weeks beforehand, I saw no reason why I should go into repertory.

It was Michaelis who broke the silence. 'Do you not fast in England and hurt your stomach before Easter?'

'Some of us do,' I said.

He pursued the question. 'Do you?' he said.

I nodded.

'What,' he asked, 'do you do?'

'Well,' I said, 'when we celebrated Easter a few weeks ago I gave up drink.'

There was a horrible sound as both Vasili and Yanni choked on their retsina. 'You did what?' said Vasili, in a voice barely above a whisper.

'I gave up drinking,' I said.

Had I said I had given up breathing the effect could not have been greater. Vasili looked at Yanni and Yanni looked at Vasili. Then they both looked at Michaelis; and then they all looked at me.

'*That*,' said Michaelis, 'is something we never do.'

'Never,' said Yanni.

'Never!' said Vasili. He was badly shaken. 'And if you have done this thing,' he continued, his eyes still filled with a mixture of horror and admiration, 'if you have made this sacrifice, then you can eat anything you wish! Sosta?'

'Sosta!' they said, 'anything! And nobody will be offended when you eat the forbidden food.'

I was much comforted by their blessing and their assurances. However, what they did not say was (a) you can eat anything you like – if you can get it, and (b) nobody is going to be offended – if they know the facts – and whilst I do not wish to dwell on the sins of omission, had they given me this additional information I should have been more prepared to face the challenge with which I was confronted on the Monday.

'Yasas! Sylvi,' I said brightly, as I went into her pastry shop for my breakfast and greeted both her and Yanni the Barber who was freshly returned from an early service in the Church, 'Yohourti me meli parakalo – yoghurt and honey please, as usual.'

Yanni drew his breath in sharply, looked quickly at Sylvi and left hurriedly for his own establishment next door.

'Yohourti?' said Sylvi, as if she had never heard the word. 'Yohourti? Ah, yohourti, yes. Yes, yohourti! No! There is no yohourti today. No,' she said, 'unfortunately the cow has broken down. And,' she added, not wishing to hurt my feelings by telling me the truth but at the same time leaving me in no doubt as to the future, 'I think it will be broken down until Sunday.'

I tried four establishments before I got my breakfast. Three of them apparently drew their supplies from the same cow which must have had the highest milk yield in or out of the EEC, and the seller to the fourth had been taken ill with a mysterious malady and was unlikely to recover before the end of the week. In the fifth, presumably owned by a Dissenter, I met with success: I did get my yoghurt. Unfortunately my own Lenten penance and my subsequent dispensation had not reached everyone.

Sitting opposite to me, dunking bread into his coffee and addressing himself unenthusiastically to a bowl of olives, was a dear little man named Kosta. We had exchanged greetings when I went in – not in the conventional way, but by saying 'Aah!' to each other. We employed this form of salutation because not only was Kosta deaf, but apart from being able to say 'Aah', he was also mute. He was also very devout, and many a time in the early summer and the autumn we had waved to each other through the incense in church. We were on very good terms and continued to be so – until the arrival of my yoghurt.

I had not taken more than a spoonful when I heard a 'plop'. Looking up I saw that Kosta's bread had dropped from his outraged fingers into his milkless coffee. 'Ah!' he said, and shook his fist at me. 'Ah!' he repeated, as he shot to his feet, knocking his chair over as he did so; and swiftly crossed to my table. 'Ah!' he re-affirmed, pointing to my yoghurt like an avenging angel. And then to make quite certain I had got the message he pointed toward Heaven with another 'Aah!', drew his finger across his throat; and emptied my yoghurt into my lap. 'Aah!' he said.

Shortly afterwards, and still smelling unpleasantly of sour milk, I met my panel of advisers and told them of the incident. 'Ah, yes,' they said, 'Kosta! Yes, that is difficult but we will do our best – come with us.'

I watched them in their attempts to tell Kosta of my virtue. I do not think they were successful. After an indifferent display of mime in which all three of them raised imaginary glasses up and down to their lips in rapid succession, at the same time pressing their hands together in prayer and looking upward and shaking their heads, I was convinced, if Kosta was not, that I was an alcoholic and beyond redemption. At all events, despite their efforts, it was some while before diplomatic relations were restored between the two of us.

On the whole most of Kardamena kept rigidly to the daily intake of fruit, salads, olives, bread and squid, and by the end of the period of abstinence one could hear the village reverberating to the sound of rumbling stomachs. This low protein diet, which was washed down by the permitted and un-interrupted flow of alcohol, also resulted in many of the faithful reacting slowly to the events of the day and walking as if on cotton wool. However, not everyone was as devout nor as strict as Kosta, and I did notice that quite a number of the less strong minded went to the wall by only the second day. Vasili was of their number: but he fell by the wayside on the evening of the first.

Michaelis's that night was crammed full of soldiers sombrely getting outside platefuls of potatoes with the odd defector surreptitiously eating a meatball. Michaelis himself was drinking herb tea from a glass, Yanni the Bicycle was staring lugubriously at a pile of greens, Yacobus the Agricultural Police was making heavy weather of some squid, and somewhat self-consciously I was supping off fried fish behind a propped-up book on my table by the lavatory door. From time to time patrons en route for that establishment would halt with their hands on the door handle, lick their lips as they took in my menu, disappear, and then repeat the procedure on their way back.

Although technically I was within my rights, which nobody challenged directly, I began to develop a guilt complex; gradually the fish before me turned to sawdust and I pushed it from me. As I did so there was a great commotion in the street, the glass doors of the taverna burst open with a crash and there stood Vasili. He was very drunk.

'Yasas – oli mazee!' he roared, flinging his arms wide open and embracing the world, 'Good evening everybody! I have news for you!'

There was an expectant silence. 'I have,' said Vasili, allowing his arms to fall down, 'just drunk a bottle of whisky, and,' he continued, raising his arm and killing the outbreak of applause, 'I have eaten . . . two platefuls of souvlaki! Not one plateful –

but two! And what is more,' he bellowed defiantly, bringing his peroration to a close, 'I do not care!' And then to a chorus of Tck! tck! tck! from the potato eaters and Bravo! Bravo! from the meatballers he weaved his way to my table, embraced me, and ordered a bottle of retsina.

He was still amazingly articulate when five empty bottles stood between us, but just as he was about to order the sixth I put my hand on his arm.

'Vasili, my friend,' I said, 'don't you think you have drunk enough?'

'Oche!' he said, 'Oche! It is nothing! Do you know, Yanni, I once drank sixteen bottles of retsina! Ne! Sosta, Yanni, sosta! True! Sixteen bottles!'

'*Sixteen?*' I said. 'But didn't you have a headache when you woke up?'

'Oche!' he said, 'No! no! no! – no headache – I was very well.' He paused. 'But,' he said, 'I did sleep for two days.'

I think history must have repeated itself that night for I did not see him again until the evening service on the Friday, but I was told that when Poppi his wife saw him, on her return from the church where she had been swinging on the bell rope and tolling the sober to prayer, her wrath was horrible to behold. Her anger was not aroused because Vasili had had one or five bottles too many – Poppi herself was not averse to having a sip at the hard stuff during those debilitating days to ensure that the bell should ring strongly – but because he had eaten meat and, moreover, bragged about his sin, publicly.

That week leading to Easter Day was an eventful one, and I have rejoiced many times since that I was in Kardamena then. Every day one saw preparations of some kind taking place. I remember looking down on to the street from the roof of Kosta's pension on the Tuesday and watching the women, young and old, carrying enormous yard-square black baking trays full of uncooked pastries. These were the biscota pascalina, the Easter biscuits, honey sweet when they were cooked and shaped in plaits and curls and elaborate twists, and alphas and omegas.

The trays weighed a ton. I had first-hand experience of that fact because I was pressed into service to carry them, and despite all my endeavours I never did manage to do what the women did and bear two trays at once, one on either side of the body, each resting on a hip. It must have been very tiring for them but they coped and made their way with them in twos and threes to the heat of the bakery at the end of the street, where they queued and awaited their turn until a perspiring Yanni the Baker took the trays from them and put them in his oven. Then back they would come, down the street in line abreast with rolled up sleeves and reddened arms, gossiping as they walked. Later, much later, they would make a return journey to the bakery and come back with the pastries golden brown and oh! – the whole street smelt of freshly baked Easter biscuit.

There were also the 'teropita', circular cheese-pies about half an inch thick. Load after load of those were carted to and from Yanni's on that Tuesday and Wednesday; and the women who were not thus engaged were busy hard-boiling eggs and dyeing them in reds and greens and yellows and blues. The shells of some were decorated with the most exquisite and delicate transfers of leaves, and everywhere I went that week I was given one but with strict instructions not to break it before Easter Day.

It was on the Tuesday that the goats and lambs arrived in the village. I watched them being unloaded from a truck. They were dumped unceremoniously in doorways or in front of shops, hogtied and bleating. As the morning wore on their cries lessened and their numbers thinned as they were taken to the Square end of the village where the butcher's shop was. They reappeared later either entire but naked and slung across the backs of cyclists or jointed and bloody in blue polythene bags; and another smell wafted through the streets of Kardamena as the skins were hung out to dry. It was all rather basic. Too basic for an English visitor I met that evening.

She was a woman of an indeterminate number of summers who, despite all her efforts – and she had worked very hard indeed – would not readily have fooled any local shepherd into pressing her into service as a Paschal lamb. When I discovered her she was, and indeed obviously had been, and for some time, looking through a glass darkly in one of the beach tavernas. When she saw me she beckoned me to her table. 'Siddown,' she said, 'have a drink.' Reluctantly I obeyed her.

'That's goo',' she said. 'Now loo' here! D'you know why I wanna tor to you?' I shook my head. 'Cos,' she said, arresting a burp, 'you've got an animal face! An aminal face,' she repeated, disregarding the switching of consonants. 'Don' misunnerstan' me – I don' mean you *look* like an animal. No! No! No! No! No!' She waved a confused palm toward me in reassurance. 'I mean you've gotta a face that looks like it – *likes* animals.' She smiled stupidly at me. 'Do you like animals?' she asked. I nodded. 'So do I,' she said, 'but the Greeks – they don' like animals. Not a bit,' she emphasized, 'not a piddling bit! They're cruel to them, the Greeks are. Tha's wha' they are – cruel!' She stopped to top herself up.

'Have you seen those dear lil' go's and lambs and things?' I nodded again. 'An' d'you know wha' they do to them?' She paused dramatically. 'They achly *kill* them,' she said; and drew her hand across her throat. 'Tha's wha' they do – they go, Kitch! And I think its dre'ful!' She peered into her empty glass and found fresh sadness in it.

For a second she examined her glass in silence and then

jerked her head upward in horrid recollection. 'And another thing too – do you know what I saw two days ago?' There was no escape.

'Tell me,' I said.

'Two days ago,' she said, 'I saw one of them – I don't know who he was – I mean, they all look alike to me, I saw one of them, taking his octopus, his *pet* octopus,' she qualified, 'for a walk.'

'Yes,' she repeated, 'for a walk. Jus' like a dog; on a string; yes; and he was walking it along the je –, the je – where they tie the boats up, and every few yards he let it down into the sea. To wet it. An' I thought: how sweet! 'Cos they like being wet, don' they?' She looked at me for confirmation. 'Yes, that's right – wet. An' then, do you know what he did?' she asked, leaning toward me.

'I've no idea,' I said untruthfully.

'Well,' she said, 'I'll tell you!' She paused to draw strength before giving me the punch line.

'The rotten bastard,' she said, her voice breaking with maudlin emotion, 'pulled it out, swung it round his head and then – an' you won't believe this – he bashed hell out of it on the rocks!'

I did believe it. I had watched the performance often enough.

But hard though I tried, nothing would convince the lady that the squid had long been dead and that the owner was tenderising it; she left the village the next day in an aura of gin and disillusionment.

I watched her go away on the morning bus from the Square. From a near-by fig-tree a flayed goat hung from a rope, swinging gently in the breeze. Its scent, acrid and heavy, joined the pot-pourri of baking and incense drifting from the church and private censers in the houses. An old man stood looking at it.

'That is a fine animal,' he said. 'It will make good eating on Sunday – better than sheep.'

'Yeti?' I asked, 'Why?'

'Because,' he said, 'it is less fatty and better for old men like me with arthritis.'

I walked out of the village and into the fields and lunched off black olives and bread in a byre with a farmer named Yanni and his wife Maria. Together we sat on upturned buckets and dipped into a communal tin.

'Tomorrow,' he said, 'you will be at church – ne?'

'Ne,' I said. 'And you?'

'Of course,' he said. 'Tomorrow is when they put the nails through Him.'

It was a crudely expressed thought; but it remained in my memory longer than many sermons. And so has the gesture of his wife.

Growing close to the byre in which we ate was a bush of Christ's thorn. As I left she stooped down, plucked a flower from it and pressed it into my shirt. 'There!' she said, 'Christ's blood is in those petals; and look!'

She pointed to the centre of the tiny red flower. In it was a droplet of moisture. 'You see?' she said. 'One of His tears which he sheds for all of us.'

I am not over-emotional, but as I turned away from them I had to blink away one of my own.

CHAPTER V

Christos Anesti! and Farewell

IN THE LATE afternoon of the Wednesday of Easter Week I saw the bereaved of the village, the black-shrouded widows making their way down the street en route for the mile-long journey to the cemetery. Some I knew: like fat full-bosomed Chrissi, who worked in Stelio's kitchen. Chrissi with her nun-white face whose husband had been drowned quite close to the shore not two years past. Her grief was still fresh. So was that of Mama Adam, whose man had died last spring. For others, time had blunted the initial pain of sadness; but all remembered.

Each carried a wreath of mauve and white plastic blooms and a spray of real flowers – the huge white arum lilies carefully grown and nurtured for that very purpose – which they would put on the graves, then trim the wicks of the tombs' night-light candles, say a prayer in front of a photograph of their dead and then return to the living community.

Some would go to church that evening; others would stay at home with their thoughts; but none would be alone. The elderly are not left in loneliness and obscurity in Kardamena. Each family looks after its own until they too are rowed by

Charon across the Styx. Old-fashioned though the word may be, there is a 'togetherness' there.

That facet of life was particularly noticeable during that week, when, with very few exceptions, all went to church on the Thursday, Friday and Saturday. Doubtless the degree of piety varied, but the rule was observed and at some time or another most put in an appearance during the three-and-a-half-hour long services. However, there were exceptions to the rule; and one such absentee was Pooh.

Pooh was not his real name, but by the end of only my second visit he answered to it. I called him Pooh because he looked like Pooh and behaved like Pooh and, as I had discovered, long words did puzzle him. He was large and he was fat. He had a Pooh-shaped nose and button eyes which were, I am sure, attached to wires, and a general Teddy-bear shape. But he was not unintelligent – far from it; nor was he lacking in shrewdness. After knowing him for only a month it became obvious to me that he had discovered the secret of living without working.

I only ever saw him do four things requiring effort: walking, sitting, spitting and yawning; and all these actions were performed in slow motion; especially yawning. Pooh's yawns were ten-second set pieces and provided a remarkable spectacle: when he opened his mouth one was privy to a graveyard with a single tombstone. Within, one saw a solitary tooth hanging proudly like a gold tipped stalactite until, with the completion of the act it disappeared again.

Everything that Pooh did was in slow-motion. When he sat down he would lower himself gently on to the seat as if he sensed it held an invisible egg; but he was a very gentle person. I used to see him, day after day, dressed in a ginger-brown cardigan over a pyjamas jacket, hands thrust deep into his trouser pockets or clasped behind his back, and with his huge feet encased in sandals bound together with yellow twine, ponderously walking with measured steps, his face toward the ground, thinking and walking, walking and thinking.

Of what he thought I have no idea; unless it was honey; like Pooh he was very fond of honey. Or it may have been his feet. They were not the greatest; like those of the unlamented Gog, they did give him cause for concern and, as I found out on the Thursday morning, particularly with regard to his religious activities.

He was having a think outside Yanni the Barber's when I came upon him, and it was really only a conversational gambit which made me ask him if he was going to church that evening.

He looked at me from under eyelids heavy with sleep and opened and shut them slowly. 'Aah,' he said; and yawned prodigiously. 'Oche! No, not tonight, Yanni. No. You see, Yanni, it is my feet! Katalavis? You understand – my feet!'

I looked blank. 'No,' I said, 'I do not understand.'

Pooh looked at me wearily, sighed, and resigned himself to giving a fuller explanation.

'You see, Yanni,' he said, 'in winter I wear shoes. Not sandals like these, but shoes – then I go to church. But in the spring and the summer, Yanni, I wear sandals and I cannot go to church because my feet get cold.'

'Then why,' I asked, 'can you not change into your shoes tonight?'

He looked sadly, first at me, and then for a long time at his unlovely feet, as if expecting an answer from them. Clearly he thought this was one below the belt. 'Because,' he said, 'because!' and turned and walked slowly away. Four paces from me he stopped. For a second he remained motionless and then turned to face me. I could see that he was an inspired Pooh.

'Because,' he said, 'my feet swell in my sandals, and become

gently on to the seat

too big for my shoes!' As I said, he was no fool. But it was well known that he and the papas were not the closest of friends.

As I watched Pooh plodding down the street, immersed in his thoughts of feet and priests, Michaelis rode toward me on his bicycle. 'Yasas!' he said as he dismounted, 'I am glad to see you. Tonight, you will eat with us, ne?' I nodded. 'Good,' he said. 'But not later than six o'clock – at half past six we finish. To go to the church. Endaxi? All right?'

'Endaxi,' I said.

'And, Yanni,' he said, propping his machine against the wall, 'only one bottle tonight – one cannot pray properly after five . . .'

At a quarter past six that evening Poppi took her first pull at the bell rope, and in ones and twos the first worshippers started to make their ways to church. By the time I took my place at seven o'clock there were thirty or so present listening to the bass, magnificent melancholy of the choir as, on their Holy and Great Thursday, they sang the litany of the Crucifixion.

As they sang, filling the church with sadness and passion and with ever-increasing power, so the numbers grew and grew until, with the building reverberating to the sound of nails being hammered home as the judicial murder of Christ was re-enacted, it had swollen to bursting point. Then, as the great black cross with the crudely painted, almost garish figure of Christ stretched upon it was raised and carried to the centre of the church, and the choir's voices were raised to a new peak of lamentation, so wreath after wreath of plastic flowers was hung upon it until the outstretched arms and bloodied head could be seen no longer. Men and women, I remember, pressed forward to kiss the effigy's feet, some dry-eyed and others weeping.

I remember, too, the airlessness; the pungency of incense; the stifling heat from the black shrouded candelabra and the hand-held candles of the sweating congregation: we were packed like sardines. Farmers and shepherds, taverna owners and fishermen, policemen and soldiers, shopkeepers and merchants, children in arms fighting to keep awake, old men who had lost count of their Easters and confessions – all were there: it was all very emotional.

When the service was over I walked to a taverna on the front together with its owner. She opened up for me and brought me a drink. Gradually others drifted in. She switched on the television and in silence her audience sat and watched a service from Athens. She gave me an egg when I left. It was blue and had a yellow flower traced on it. 'Two more days,' she said – 'Kalinichta!'

As I walked back to Kosta's the sea was as quiet and calm as a millpond. It was almost as if it too felt the need of silence.

The next evening I went to church again. Once again we stood shoulder to shoulder in the sweltering heat and again emotions were very high. The cross had gone and in its place was a stretched gold-trimmed red velvet cloth. Mounted upon it were pictures of the dead Christ and His mourners – Mary His Mother, John the Beloved, Joseph of Arimathea and Mary Magdalene. A seemingly never ending queue moved forward to kiss the faces of the figures and an elderly man with a miniature bottle of Beefeater gin filled with water took it to the papas to be blessed. Then, as the service ended, each of us holding a lighted candle and headed by the papas and the choir, followed the ornate bier of Christ from the church and processed slowly through the village.

I kept company with them for a while and then broke away to have a bird's-eye view of the scene from Kosta's roof and saw, not a column of people, but a thousand fireflies. Ten minutes later I became one of them again, and as we wended our way through the narrow streets, from the doorways of houses on either side, women splashed us with rosewater and called out blessings on us – 'Yasas! Yasas!' – and so we moved on until the whole of Kardamena had been walked.

Near to midnight I fell out and leaned against the corner of a house. Gradually the flickering candles moved out of sight and the voices of the choir grew fainter and fainter as the papas led them back to the church. From its belfry the bell tolled again as Poppi pulled at the rope for the last time that day. Twelve times it rang and then it, too, was silent. Suddenly Kardamena became very quiet.

I walked slowly back toward the pension. A cat flashed its green eyes at me as it scuttled across my path on an urgent journey, but that was the only movement I saw, and the only sound I heard was the lapping of the waves. Kosta's was in darkness when I arrived and climbed the stairs to my room. There, by my bed, I found a plate of plaited biscota pascalina, two eggs – one red, one yellow, a cheese-pie, a bottle of wine, and some flowers. I was very touched; but I was also very foolish. I ate the cheese-pie.

The name of the maker was Anastasi. She was Kosta's wife and a sweet, merry-eyed young woman she was, but while in no way casting aspersions on the excellence of her day-to-day cooking it must be said that cheese-pie making was not her forte; and I speak with some authority.

I became a connoisseur of teropita – not because I wished to do so but because I had no option. Every housewife had baked them and every day until I left I was given one to eat and some to take away. At one time I had amassed a collection of twenty-seven, half of which I took into the fields and scattered amongst the cows where, being the shape and colour they are, they did not look out of place; but I was still left with eleven at the end of my visit. One I brought back with me to England and fed it to some ducks on the Regent's Canal. I do not know whether they actually sank because I did not wait to see but by the time I left they were certainly low in the water. However, in the small hours of that Saturday morning my own personal teropita dropped into my stomach like a stone and by six o'clock it was having a pitched battle with whatever else was in residence.

There was nothing for it: I got up, took a liberal dose of anti-dyspepsia tablets, dressed, and still in grave discomfort went into the street.

I was not the first early riser. Yanni the Bicycle was abroad and so was Mama Adam who kept the taverna next door. 'Kalimera Yanni,' they said, 'have a cheese-pie'; so did Sylvi the Pastry who was sweeping her pavement; so did Michaelis and Oolah farther down the street; and so did fat Athena at the end of the road. I had collected seven by the time I reached the end of the village and my face was grey and drawn with anticipation; but it was within that dusty triangle of ground where the almirithra trees grew in clumps and stretched down to the sea that I was brought to halt by what I saw.

To my left, and quite close at hand, was a trio of tethered goats. A man, his shirt sleeves rolled to his elbows and accompanied by two small children, came toward them from a nearby clump of trees. He selected one of the goats and led it a little way from the others.

Quickly and expertly, he cut its throat. The little boy helped him to hang it by its back legs from a tree and the little girl brought her father a bowl of water. He turned it pink with his knife and hands, dried them, lit a cigarette and started to skin the animal. The episode had happened very quickly but it had been dramatic in its suddenness and had engrossed me completely; but as the butcher got to work I took in the scene as a whole.

All around, goats and sheep were being slaughtered, suspended from trees and then flayed, the whole family helping with the operation. Every tree supported one and around every tree there sat an expectant and patient, silent salivating circle of cats and dogs, their natural enmity subdued by a common rejoicing that they were not goats and secondly that they would not have to wait until the morrow to get at the offal. And as they licked their lips, watching and waiting for the viscera to be thrown to them, the other tethered candidates for the knife showed no concern – there was no unrest among them: unconcernedly they carried on cropping while their former companions had their throats cut. It was all rather biblical somehow; but I was glad to move away from the smell of blood.

Still clasping my cheese-pies I retraced my steps through the village. Two little girls aged six or seven, one in pink the other in blue, sat cross-legged and facing each other in a doorway, each holding a painted egg. 'En-a! the-o! tre-a!' they chanted, 'Christos Anesti!' and banged the points of their eggs together. Blue was the winner, and she squealed with joy as she held up her unbroken egg in triumph for me to see and then toppled backward gurgling with unbridled delight.

As I repassed Sylvi's I looked through the door and saw Yanni the Barber; but it was not the Yanni I knew. It was a forlorn Yanni I saw, a shopsoiled Yanni who was sitting forward in a chair and looking as if the end of the world had come; and he was pinker than usual. I went in.

'Yasas Yanni!' I said, 'ti kanete – how are you?'

He looked up at me from between cupped hands. 'Ya,' he croaked. His voice was a husk.

I looked inquiringly at Sylvi who was boiling water by the sink.

'It is the singing,' she said. 'Four hours a day for three days. It is too much. He will never sing again. And even if he does,' she said, grudgingly allowing the possibility of such a miracle, 'what of tonight – what of the great service tonight?' She poured the water on to some menthol crystals in the enamel bowl and took it to him. 'Sniff,' she said, 'sniff deeply'; and put a towel over his head. 'This is what the doctor has advised. But I do not think it does good; it just makes him smell.'

There was a spluttering from under the towel and Yanni emerged puce and boiled and with streaming eyes. 'Surely,' he whispered, 'there must be another way?' And looked at me imploringly.

'Wait,' I said; and went to my room. I am not a hypochondriac but I never travel without a small medicine bag. I returned with a packet of evil-looking throat pastilles which rejoiced in the name of Fisherman's Friend, a bottle of glycerine and thymol mixture and a plastic nasal inhaler.

'Here!' I said, 'suck these, gargle with this and,' I said, as politely as I could, 'stick this up your nose.' When I left him he was on his third Fisherman's Friend and looking like a one-tusked walrus with the plastic inhaler protruding from his left nostril.

When I went by the shop at midday on my way for a swim I heard the sound of heavy gargling coming from within – too heavy for a solo performance. Glancing in I saw that Yanni had been joined at the sink by two other choir members. I could not tell whether my nasal inhaler was being passed from nose to nose but my other prophylactics were certainly put to communal use. When I returned from the beach two hours later they were sitting round a table, conversing in mime, and sucking in unison.

I had no way of knowing whether it was the therapeutics which won the day or if it was a victory for auto-suggestion – perhaps it was a combination of the two, but the singing of the choir that night surpassed anything that had gone before.

The service was magnificent. It began at ten-thirty and an hour later you could not have put a knife-blade between us. Minute by minute more and more tried to join us but could not gain admittance and had to be content with listening to the service through loudspeakers outside. Toward the latter part, women, and men, pushed and stumbled past other worshippers as they struggled to get to the doors for air. In front of me the head of a young woman flopped forward as she fainted but was held up by the sheer pressure of her neighbours' bodies. Gently and gradually she was eased toward the side door, where she sat with others on the stone floor of the porch and recovered.

Near midnight the singing reached a crescendo. The papas, robed in all the splendour and richness of the Easter trappings of the Orthodox Church, swung his censer and poured out his blessings, the excitement in the congregation mounted and then, on the stroke of twelve, in a solid, sweating, chattering phalanx we left the church and went outside; and as the papas, followed by the choir, reached the top of the flight of stone steps leading to the church's gallery and cried with outstretched arms: 'Christos Anesti! – Christ is risen!' so the night sky erupted and exploded in a display and cannonade of fireworks.

'Christos Anesti!' cried everyone, 'Christos Anesti!' and embraced the nearest to them for this was the Meres Agapis – the Day of Love. Everyone kissed everyone! Fat old women I had waved to in the fields, modest young ones who had hitherto been shy, Vasilis and Kostas and Yannis and Yiorgos – all surged in a sea of emotion and kissed me and each other as if none of us would meet again for a thousand years. And all the while the mortars and the roman candles banged their salutes in fiery fountains and the rockets seared the sky. Then, arm-in-arm, we dispersed to various houses to have the traditional Soup of the Day. I am not sure of its ingredients but I was told that it was made from split lamb's head and garlic; certainly the latter was present. It was an acquired taste, but as the embracing continued enthusiastically throughout the day was glad I had had some.

I got to bed at three o'clock that Easter morning full of teropita and soup, but even during those early hours I was given a clear indication of how the rest of the day would be spent. After a week's abstinence the shrunken tums of Kardamena were going to be filled.

I had four hours' sleep that night. Just before seven I was awakened by a noise from outside. As in a trance I staggered to the balcony and exhaled a cloud of garlic seaward. Below me in the alleyway was the source of the disturbance. It was Kosta. He was singing and doing a little dance with some scrawny six-week-old chickens. He had a bottle in one hand, a teropita in the other, and he was very happy.

'Ah, Yanni!' he shouted, when he saw the horrid sight above him, 'Christos Anesti! – have a cheese-pie!' And hurled his own toward me like a discus. It missed me and ricocheted off the wall. 'And do not forget,' he said, ignoring the fragments which rained upon him like manna, creating hysteria among the chickens, 'do not forget, simera – todai, you do naut sai, "kalimera". Oche! Todai you sai – "Christos Anesti!" because thees es the dai when the Jesus-man went hup! Katalavis?'

'Katalava,' I said. I understood perfectly.

'And do naut forget also,' he continued from the midst of his berserk brood, 'that todai you kiss aul the baudies, todai you lauve aul the baudies – even if you hate them! Yes! Avrio – tomorrow, tomorrow you can hate them again with pleasure!'

He was a splendid chap; but I was glad he had missed me

with his teropita because between the hours of eight and twelve
I was forced to sample seven. All came from different places
of origin and all were of varying degrees of excellence and
texture. I felt like an adjudicator at a Women's Institute
Cookery Competition, and by eleven-thirty not only was my
digestive system under strain but my diplomacy as well.

From house to house I went. 'Um. Yes!' I said, 'Delicious!
Um! – kala! Yes! What? Oh yes! – *just* as good as Athena's,
yes. Whose? Oh *hers*! Oh yes, well – ha! ha! ha!, no comparison
at all, no, yours are much bet – pardon! – much better . . .'

As the marathon progressed, I became more and more dis-
comfited by the thought that at noon I was to present myself
and my leaden stomach at Vasili's and Poppi's for lunch; but
at eleven forty-five, and holding a red rose and two teropita
which were given to me lest I should feel faint en route, I left
my last port of call and made my way to their house.

As I have hinted, Vasili was an unusual man; and so was
his house. Indeed, going into the Vasili menage was not unlike
entering an underwater cave, a Poseidon's grotto. It was
decorated almost entirely with dried sponges, petrified driftwood, old urns and limpet-encrusted wine jars and stone
bottles, coral and seaweed, and scallop-shell ashtrays: one half-
expected Poppi to appear, all seventeen stone of her, balancing
on a fishtail and waving a trident. And it was in that setting that
we were joined by Vasili's son and his wife and their two small
boys, and sat down to Easter dinner at a table which had an
exquisite five-stemmed branch of coral draped with seaweed
for a centre-piece and which groaned under the weight of food.

I shall not forget that meal. Poppi said grace from behind a
wash tub of goat, and there was a moment's silence as we all
made the sign of the cross. What followed was remarkable.
Somewhere an imaginary whistle blew, the tapes went up and
we were off.

'Christos Anesti!' we cried as we banged hell out of each other's hard boiled eggs, scattered the shells and stampeded through a plateful.

'Isighia!' roared Vasili through a yellow blanket of yolk, as they drowned in retsina and were garnished with onions.

'Bravo!' burped Poppi as the goat went down.

'Kala!' said her son to a mountain of rice.

'Ne! Ne!' screamed the boys in reply to their mother.

'Ya!' yelled Vasili, as more bottles appeared.

And 'Oh no,' I moaned, when the cucumber and chocolate appeared simultaneously – 'Oh no! no! no!' But it was of little use: one was not allowed to refuse.

I think it was three hours later that I left, sweating profusely. But one fact I do remember: when I left Poppi was topping up with cheese-pie; but I had a very light meal that evening.

Two days later I left Kardamena – a year and a day since I first set foot in it with the dreadful Gogs on the eve of May Day. On the night before my departure I supped with most of my friends in Michaelis's taverna. 'Tried and True' I had dubbed it, and tried and true it was – like the people of the village. The meal, as they say, was on the house.

I did not go to bed directly when I returned to Kosta's. Instead I went on to the roof for a last look around and watched Kardamena go to sleep. At my back was the sound of the sea and around me the singing of cicadas. The streets were almost empty. Four young men talking politics argued their way toward the Square, halted, shook hands, split up, and went off two by two. A soldier, shaven-headed, crossed uncertainly in front of me, his face glowing as he drew on his cigarette, and then passed on and out of sight; and in the taverna on my left Mama Adam put out her lights, one by one, and two elderly cleaners guided each other into the rectangular shadows. Kardamena was almost spent; but not quite. From somewhere in the distance there was the sound of bouzoukoi music. I knocked out my pipe, went into the street again, walked along the beach toward it, and then stood, listening.

Footsteps crunched on the shingle behind me. It was Vasili. 'I thought it was you,' he said; and lit a cigarette. There was silence, and then he said:

'You are sad to be going?'

'Ne,' I said, quietly.

'And we are sad, too,' he said, 'for now you are one of us; but you will return – again you will return?'

'Ne,' I said.

'Good,' he said, 'very good; Kardamena is a good village, Yanni – sosta?'

'Sosta,' I said, 'true.'

He left me by his house. 'Kalinichta, Yanni mu,' he said, 'Good night, my Yanni,' and embraced me. I did not see him again before I left.

Next morning Dimitri drove me to the airport. There were only a few travellers waiting in the tiny departure lounge. Among them was an English girl who had been in Kardamena for months. She sat at a table facing a young lieutenant in the Army. Between them were two untouched cups of coffee.

They sat in silence. He stared at the table and she at a small gold crucifix which she held in her fingers. I turned away from them lest she should sense I was looking at them and could see that her cheeks were wet. I was not the only one to be leaving the village with a heavy heart.

As we crossed over the coast and the familiar landmarks became harder and harder to see, I thought again of Vasili's words the previous evening. 'Kardamena is a good village, Yanni – sosta?'

It is: a good village and a good community; but I have fears for its future – as a community; I have watched it grow and in the little space of two years I have seen it change and I think it may well suffer the fate of all Greek villages once they have been 'discovered'. Two springs ago there was no discotheque – there is now; and there is a supermarket and two souvenir shops with signs in English and German pointing toward them; and Yanni the Bicycle has mopeds for hire. And when I left last time I counted eight new buildings and saw roofs untidy with bent metal rods looking like walking sticks in conference – the foundations for other storeys; and I watched and heard cement-laden lorries go rumbling down the main street to where an hotel is being built two kilometres away. The locals say that it will never be finished – that it will become another sepulchre like the one at Kephelos further down the coast, the one inspired by Papoudoupoulos when he was in power – 'And in any case, Yanni, it will not affect us – oche!'

I hope they are right. I hope the day will not come when Kardamena becomes another village geared solely to the tourist; where the fishing nets are used only as ornaments and the young and not-so-young no longer dance as their fancy takes them but to an ordered choreography. I hope they are right and that my fears will be proved groundless. But no matter what architectural changes take place whilst those folk about whom I have written are alive I shall always return, in the quiet of the year, to see them; for they are the salt of the earth.

I do not know conclusively what draws me to the islands. Perhaps it is because in the Greek islander I find a measure of myself. They are extrovert and inclined to extremes of mood; prone to laziness and industry in turn; lovers of high drama and exaggeration; and they laugh readily and cry easily. Perhaps it is these traits which helped me to become enamoured of them. Or perhaps it was their overt kindness and willingness to give and help which made me embrace them, for nowhere in the world have I been in receipt of such warmth as I was given by the men and women of the villages of Andros and Kos.

Among them I have found timelessness and with it that most prized and most elusive of all desires. Peace.